Praise for *Church Planting Wife*

With all the church planting we see today, we often overlook the calling and the burden that is placed on the woman behind the man. Christine Hoover's vivid storytelling of the struggles and joys of being a church planter's wife is beautifully woven into God's truth for women who find themselves under the difficult task of ministering to the man who ministers to everyone else.

> —MATT CARTER, church planter and pastor of Preaching and Vision at the Austin Stone Community Church, coauthor with Darrin Patrick of *For the City: Proclaiming and Living Out the Gospel*

Few things are as challenging and exciting as planting a church. This book will help you get through the tough times and help you appreciate the blessings in church planting.

> —LORA BATTERSON, wife of Mark Batterson, who planted and pastors National Community Church in Washington D.C.

Church planting wives, you will feel that Christine Hoover has read your journals. She is on your journey and is able to verbalize church planting skillfully and with penetrating honesty. This is a must-read book. You have found the mentor you have longed for.

> —KATHY FERGUSON LITTON, national consultant for Ministry Wives, North American Mission Board

Across the globe the priorities of a church planting wife are the same: love the Lord, love your husband and family, love the church. Christine invites you into her life and the lives of other women as they have Christ-centered conversations about seeking to live out their privileged calling wherever God has planted them.

> —GLORIA FURMAN, church planting wife in the Middle East, author of *Glimpses of Grace: Treasuring the Gospel in Your Home*

Too often we, as church planters' wives, have suffered in silence as we've battled criticism, isolation, or discouragement in ministry. Christine not only shares the raw emotions that come with the difficulties of church planting, she gives much-needed insight for flourishing in ministry for a lifetime. *The Church Planting Wife* will not disappoint!

> —TRICIA LOVEJOY, wife of Shawn Lovejoy, who is the founder and pastor of Mountain Lake Church in Atlanta, GA and the founder of Churchplanters.com

D0018764

Ministry is both a challenge and a blessing. The demands of responsibility can eat away the joy of changed lives. This is especially true in the heart of a church planting wife, but it doesn't have to be. We have known Christine long before she had the job description of Church Planting Wife. In the past and present, we have seen her faith shine! In these pages she will help your faith shine as well. You are on an exciting journey; let Christine walk with you as you embrace your role as a church planting wife.

> —GREGG and KELLY MATTE, pastor and wife of Houston's First Baptist Church, Founder of Breakaway Ministries at Texas A&M, author of *I AM changes who I am.*

Church planting is not an endeavor pursued in isolation. Husbands cannot succeed in ministry without their wives and vice versa. I am delighted Christine has put together this helpful resource to encourage church planting wives.

> —ED STETZER, president of LifeWay Research and author of *Planting Missional Churches*

The church planting wife—what goes on in her heart? It's an all-encompassing spiritual and emotional pendulum swinging from fear to trust and every emotion in between. Christine's vulnerable insights will encourage you amidst the heart-swings, offering a steady hold on peace in the God who called you. I've been deeply blessed by these truth-filled words after my eight years on the planting journey.

> —GINGER VASSAR, wife of JR Vassar, who is founder and pastor of Apostles Church in New York City

This honest, powerful, wonderfully written book is a must-read for every church planting wife. Christine gives all planting wives the gift of knowing they are not alone in the struggles and challenges they face. She also offers them the hope they need to continue on in serving God in their churches.

> —LORI WILHITE, founder of Leading and Loving It and wife of Jud Wilhite, who is senior pastor at Central Christian Church in Las Vegas

Christine's real-life approach to ministry makes her contagious. She honestly shares the ups and downs of church planting while offering encouragement that provides hope. *The Church Planting Wife* is a handbook for ladies who are beginning this journey as well as seasoned church planting wives.

> —BRANDI WILSON, wife of Pete, who is pastor of Cross Point Church in Nashville, TN. Brandi is the coauthor of *Leading and Loving It.*

THE CHURCH PLANTING WIFE

HELP *and* HOPE *for*
HER HEART

Christine Hoover

MOODY PUBLISHERS
CHICAGO

Published in association with the literary agency of Les Stobbe, 300 Doubleday Road, Tryon, NC 28782.

All Scripture quotations, unless otherwise indicated, are taken from the *New King James Version*. Copyright © 1982 by Thomas Nelson, Inc. Used by permission. All rights reserved.

Scripture quotations marked ESV are taken from *The Holy Bible, English Standard Version*. Copyright © 2000, 2001 by Crossway Bibles, a division of Good News Publishers. Used by permission. All rights reserved.

Scripture quotations marked NIV are taken from the *Holy Bible, New International Version*®, NIV®. Copyright © 1973, 1978, 1984 by Biblica, Inc.™ Used by permission of Zondervan. All rights reserved worldwide. www.zondervan.com

Scripture quotations marked NRSV are taken from the New Revised Standard Version Bible, copyright © 1989 National Council of the Churches of Christ in the United States of America. Used by permission. All rights reserved.

Scripture quotations marked THE MESSAGE are from *The Message*, copyright © by Eugene H. Peterson 1993, 1994, 1995. Used by permission of NavPress Publishing Group.

All emphasis to Scripture has been added by the author.

Edited by Pam Pugh   Interior Design: Julia Ryan/www.DesignByJulia.com
Cover Design: faceout®studio Cover Image: Shutterstock #68995447, #59343640

Library of Congress Cataloging-in-Publication Data
Hoover, Christine.
  The church planting wife : help and hope for her heart / Christine Hoover.
     p. cm.
  Includes bibliographical references.
  ISBN 978-0-8024-0638-5
  1. Church development, New. 2. Missionaries' spouses--Biography.
3. Christian women--Biography. I. Title.
BV652.24.H66 2013
253'.22—dc23

                                                        2012029670

Moody Publishers
820 N. LaSalle Boulevard
Chicago, IL 60610

1 3 5 7 9 10 8 6 4 2

Printed in the United States of America

*For Kyle, who makes me an
incredibly happy church planting wife.*

Contents

"Therefore, my beloved (sisters), be steadfast, immovable, always abounding in the work of the Lord, knowing that your labor is not in vain in the Lord."
1 Corinthians 15:58

Am I Willing?

npacking in our new home in a new state far from our families, I opened a box marked *Fragile* with big black letters. Inside, buried under bubble wrap, I found my framed wedding vows. While I searched the master bedroom for the perfect spot where the frame could hang, I read what I had committed to Kyle on our wedding day. Just as it had when I had first written the words, my heart stopped on one line.

I vow to support the ministry that God gives you.

My husband and I wrote those wedding vows in Steamboat Springs, Colorado, on a trip with my future in-laws just weeks before our big day. Outside, snow blanketed the ground and inside, armed with two spiral notebooks, Kyle and I sat purposefully to write the words we would covenant with each other for life.

As soon I put pen to paper, the weight of the task gripped me, calling for all the wisdom I could muster. But none came.

I thought.

I took a drink of water.

I thought some more.

After staring at the blank spiral notebook page for twenty long minutes, I questioned the conviction that we should write our own vows. What to write? How does a twenty-three-year-old girl understand what a marriage commitment entails, much less express it in words, words that will be spoken as a promise before God and people? I couldn't slap down a string of loving sentiments and check off another item on my wedding to-do list. Each word I considered writing took on so much weight that I could not write one at all. Remembering the sample vows the minister sent us, I pulled them from my luggage. *Oh, good,* I thought. *Something to copy.* But after plagiarizing *I, Christine,* and waiting for inspiration to follow, hesitation paralyzed me.

What do I want to commit to this man? What will I promise him?

Exasperated, I glanced at Kyle's back for clues as to what he was feverishly writing. I should have been glad his thoughts were spilling out of him like a waterfall—after all, they were meant for me—but, instead, I felt a rising irritation that my own words were not coming.

Why was this so difficult for me? My hesitation, I knew, had nothing to do with how I felt about Kyle. My certainty about him had developed over three years of dating, beginning in our final years of college and culminating in our engagement on my twenty-third birthday. Even before we started dating, when we were acquaintances, and I observed his purposeful approach to relationships, he intrigued me. He was a natural leader, quietly drawing others in by his example and vision. Other college men gathered around him with respect in their eyes; a man's man, one might say. When we began dating, he increasingly captivated me with his passion for life, his sense of humor, his humility, and especially, his gentleness toward me. I never tired of him; a lifetime felt too short a period to be his companion and know all I could know about him. Three years of dating solidified my desire for him; marrying him was only fitting. Besides, it seemed we were individually moving toward the same goals. Why not do it together? I wondered if other couples felt as happy as we did; certainly I hoped everyone experienced what I experienced with Kyle.

Reminiscing inspired me, so with pen to paper once again, I urged myself on. *What do I want to commit to this man? What will I promise him?*

After mulling my answers to those questions, I translated my thoughts into vows of commitment, words finally filling the paper:

> *I, Christine, offer myself completely to you, Kyle, to be your wife in marriage.*
> *I vow to put my relationship with Christ first in my life,*
> > *but nothing else before you,*
> *To place our home under your leadership,*
> *To place your needs above my own,*
> *To support the ministry that God gives you,*
> *And to love you with the faithfulness that God has shown me.*
> *I commit to standing beside you faithfully in all circumstances.*
> *Kyle, you are my best friend and a treasured gift from God.*
> *I dedicate our marriage and our home to the lordship of Jesus Christ*
> > *and look forward to serving Him together as one.*

I read the vows several times, each time imagining myself speaking them on our wedding day and, each time, hesitating at the promise to support Kyle's calling into ministry. Although they were weighty, the other lines felt right to me; I could confidently make those promises to Kyle. I considered scratching the ministry line because it seemed out of place for wedding vows, but my heart felt unsettled at that prospect, too. I couldn't pinpoint the difficulty surrounding this one vow. Kyle had a clear call to ministry, of which I was fully supportive. In fact, although I had rarely voiced it, I had felt a similar call on my life from the time I was in high school. I suspected I would marry someone with the same calling. When Kyle told me what he wanted to do with his life, I thought, *Well, of course!* as if it were silly to consider anything else. We rarely discussed the calling—it was a given, a natural

For the first time, I considered what ministry might mean for my life.

next step for both of us, something we were willing to give our lives for. The hesitation, then, to put my support in writing surprised me. Possibly for the first time, in the middle of writing my wedding vows, I considered what ministry might mean for my life.

At that time, we both attended seminary while Kyle also worked for a Christian men's organization. Although we'd held separate ministry leadership positions in college, we had never done ministry together, but we certainly hoped for opportunities in which we could serve side by side. In that vacation spot, as I considered the future with a moment of God-given clarity, I saw what a lifetime of ministry might entail: shouldering heavy responsibilities, giving ourselves away to others, living far away from family, or possibly enduring criticism or defeat for the sake of the gospel. Because Kyle had surrendered control of his future to God, my vow of support meant stepping into his shadow and following him where God led. Was I willing? Was my conviction so firm that I would speak those words to Kyle and to God in front of my friends and family?

Eight years after that day, I stood in our new home, holding those vows in my hands. We had just moved to Charlottesville, Virginia, to start a church from scratch. I recalled hearing the term *church planter* in seminary, but had not known what it meant, certainly not imagining the term would ever describe us. Yet there I stood, dusting off a frame of my wedding vows in a home and a city where we didn't know anyone. Although much had changed since the day we wrote our promises down on scratch paper—we had three little boys and Kyle's experience of serving on staff at a church in Texas— the same questions arose in my heart, urging for a silent renewal of the vow I had made to my husband. When I'd first said those words, they had been a general affirmation of the calling on my husband's life. Now we faced the difficult work of church planting. My support and affirmation of my husband's ministry would be crucial.

Was I willing?

CHAPTER ONE

the Heart *of the* Church Planting Wife

A fellow mom recently asked me, "What's it like being a church planter's wife?"

On my best days, when I am overwhelmed by God's grace and can imagine nothing better than the life I live, I marvel at the privilege I've been given.

The Long and the Short of It

In my darkest hours, however, when I am overcome with self-pity and a longing to be free of the calling God has placed on my life, I have formed a different answer to that question. Rather than an answer, it's more of a rehearsed soapbox speech in which I spew the self-centered grievances piled up in the corner of my heart.

She looked at me expectantly, obviously wanting the first response, the response that matched her ideal picture of ministry. Feeling guilty for my negative internal reaction, I reprimanded myself and asked, "Do you want the short answer or the long one?"

The short answer is that church planting is difficult and demanding, but tremendously rewarding.

The long answer entails much more because church planting is a lifestyle; nothing in my life goes untouched by my husband's calling. I find it challenging to describe in detail how this work affects the deep regions of my heart or even to understand it myself, both the joys of seeing God change lives through our work and the struggles of bitter disappointments and personal failures. Although our work often defies description, at times my greatest desire is for my friends, family members, our church members, and even my husband to understand the blessings, joys, frustrations, and struggles that come with being a church planting wife. I long for others to see and experience the joys in surrendering to Christ, in going on mission with Him. I want to eloquently express what it's like watching my children grow up among a body of believers who know and love them, seeing immature believers become strong and grounded in the faith, witnessing the gospel transform lives, seeing my husband flourish in his calling, and enjoying those simple moments at church when I look around in wonder at what God has allowed me to be a part of.

At the same time, I want to tell them about the intense spiritual warfare, the sense of spiritual isolation, and the self-death that is required in this work. If they could just understand, I think, they could relate to me, rejoice with me, know my needs, and somehow ease the most difficult aspects of church planting. If I'm not careful, the nature of this calling can create in me a sense of self-focus, self-pity, or isolation. Or I feel misunderstood and long for the rhythms of a "normal" life.

Sometimes I feel unsettled by my vacillation between struggle and joy. *Am I making this harder than it should be? Am I truly called to this if I wrestle with it this much?* Sometimes I grow discouraged that I am still in such a fierce battle between flesh and spirit.

Along this road, I've discovered (to my great relief) that I'm not alone in what I have experienced as a church planting wife.

As a planter's wife, I have the joy of seeing my husband filled with excitement of a calling realized and followed. I have the burden and concern of helping hold up his weary arms during a busy season of ministry infancy and bivocational physical fatigue. I'm also being refined as I have many opportunities to trust the Lord for provision financially. I am learning to keep fears and emotions in check so that in the midst of inevitable spiritual warfare, I don't become a stumbling block or discouragement to him.

On the whole, I'm thrilled to be a church planting wife. The countless joys are coupled with and balanced by refining moments and trials, and I'm grateful that this is what the Lord has for me in His plan.—Lori McDonald, Corpus Christi, TX

He Knows the Roller Coaster

Perhaps you too have thrilled at the faith-filled adventure of following God. Maybe you have felt the joy of seeing a life transformed or a marriage healed by the gospel going forth in your community. Most likely you have enjoyed the fruit God has grown through your work. But perhaps you have also never felt so vulnerable and fragile. Maybe you have been wounded, discouraged, or fearful. You may be church planting alongside your husband in a place that is far from your friends and extended family. You may feel alone without other staff members or elders to share the load in your new church. Maybe you and your husband have encountered resistance from other pastors in your area, removing any sense of camaraderie and teamwork. Possibly you have young children or are working to support your family, both of which leave little time to connect with others. Perhaps you have dealt with criticism, hurts, failure, or exhaustion. Or maybe additional pressures have compounded the challenges of church planting, like they have for our co-laborers here in Charlottesville:

Being part of a church plant helped me understand what being dependent on God feels and looks like in my everyday life. I was often discouraged, anxious, and yet had peace. During the season of early church planting, I kept thinking: "Is God really enough? If you take everything else away, would I choose God over all the comforts the world has to offer?"

My husband was diagnosed with cancer the year before we moved across the country back to our hometown to plant a church.

Within a few months of planting the church, his cancer came back. Not only were we struggling with the church plant, but we were also fighting cancer. Through the surgeries and radiation, it was hard to pray. But I could feel the power of prayer and had a peace that could only come from God. He used the people in our young church to support, care for, and feed us. God has made this part of our story, reminding us that He is always there. While we were out of commission dealing with cancer, God grew our church. He provided for our every need, and in each stage of this journey He continues to be faithful in providing for us.—Jenn Atwell

Whatever you have faced, I imagine you have felt the same roller coaster of emotions that I have in this ministry, with both its exhilaration and heart-pounding fear.

Does your heart—like mine—cry out? Does it cry out for rest, love, encouragement, friendship, provision, security, balance, for someone to shoulder the weight with you?

We have needs of the heart, and we wonder what to do or how to handle our struggles. Does anyone notice? Does anyone care? Are all the sacrifices we're making in vain?

Most people assume that church planting pastors and their wives have tamed the temptations of the heart. Certainly, they think, those who take the gospel to an unreached neighborhood or city are spiritually stable and undaunted by fear, temptation, or discouragement. As church planting wives, however, we know the truth. We know that we are like everyone else, that our hearts are prone to wander, to sin, to doubt, and to grow discouraged. We know that we are desperate and needy for Christ, our heart's ally. We feel fragile. A lot.

And He knows.

He knows that it's difficult to communicate how church planting affects us. He knows our greatest concerns, joys, fears, and disappointments. In fact, He is the *only* One who fully understands our lives and hearts. And though few people can identify with us, we should not despair. Though we can and should share our struggles with others, their understanding can only go so far. He alone knows so that we will turn to Him alone.

The Lord's knowledge of our lives isn't as an observer or spectator.

Instead, it is as a participant, as One who is intimately involved and invested in us. Others may not understand our circumstances, our lifestyle, or the inner recesses of our hearts, but thankfully, we have a forever ally in Christ who concerns Himself with our spiritual and emotional needs. When we feel so lonely that our heart aches, He knows. When we are bursting with joy, He knows. When we are weighed down by discouragement, He knows. When our hearts are at rest because of Him, He knows. When we are paralyzed by fear, He knows.

He knows.

He sees.

He cares.

And all the while He whispers to us: *Trust Me with your heart. It's safe with Me.*

This is very good news for us as church planting wives, for He stills the roller coaster of emotion. He steadies our hearts, and He enables us to fulfill this calling.

"Why Did You Bring Me Here?"

A different whisper, however, comes at the first hint of struggle in church planting: *God doesn't care. He doesn't see. He doesn't want to meet the needs of your heart. He has left you alone.* The enemy of God will challenge your heart's devotion and stir up fear in your soul.

My heart has been tested countless times throughout our church planting experience, starting from the moment I unpacked the last moving box. In the months leading up to our move, we had been asked countless times, "Just how *do* you start a church?" We had read every church planting book in existence, received counsel from seasoned church planters, and developed a clear vision of what we hoped our church would become. But when I hung the last frame on the wall, Kyle and I looked at each other and said, "*Now* what?" We didn't know a single person in our city besides our Realtor and a neighbor who had welcomed us with a plate of cookies. The challenge ahead of us seemed completely overwhelming, and I questioned our choices and our sanity. Could God really make something out of *nothing?*

Over the course of the first year, nothing came easy.

We started a Sunday evening Bible study in our home a month after moving to Charlottesville. On the first night, ten people attended, four of whom were considered church leaders, and three of whom were our children. The kids sat still for worship but then roamed in and out of the living room during Bible study, causing such a distraction that I took them upstairs and missed half of our first church gathering.

Later, after cleaning the kitchen and putting away all of the leftover cookies I had made for our guests, I retreated to our bedroom and cried. In fact, for most of the fall, my Sunday evenings looked similar to that first one: I cleaned the house, made food, greeted people, wrangled children all throughout church, mingled and said goodbye, cleaned the house again—then cried. Even into the spring, when we moved our meeting time to Sunday mornings and started to outgrow our living room, I struggled to conjure up the faith and excitement I had come to Charlottesville with. I longed for families to join us—most of our growth was from young, single people—and especially for God to make things easier and more comfortable for us.

> I wondered why we weren't the church planters who experienced explosive growth in a short period of time.

I wondered why we weren't the church planters who experienced explosive growth in a short period of time. How I envied those people.

I began putting undue pressure on Kyle because I was emotionally fragile, uncertain of my role, and lonely. Church planting was proving harder than I had originally expected. "Why did you bring me here?" I'd say to Kyle, my words dripping with resentment. He'd gently remind me that God called me here too, that we were a team, and that I'd felt so certain when we were preparing to leave Texas.

I mourned the change and what it required of me: more sacrifice, less of my husband, more uncertainty, less of the familiar routines we had once enjoyed. In my emotional need, I wanted my husband's full attention, but, tasked with a great responsibility, he had so little to give me. I grew disillusioned—with ministry, with church planting, and with marriage. I dwelled there, feeding my sinful thoughts. *What if we had* never moved here? What if Kyle hadn't gone into ministry? What if we had ignored God's call to church plant? What if I hadn't married someone in the ministry? What would it hurt just to give up?

I also aimed my bitter arrows at God. Why can't You make this easier? I have been obedient and faithful in coming here, and this is what I get?

A Heart Monitored

I had entered church planting with a firm faith, but because I didn't closely guard my heart, because I listened to those little poisonous whispers, I forgot that God loved me and I doubted His provision. Resentful, my heart hardened toward Kyle and toward God. My unwillingness to submit to the Lord and accept His good purposes for me made it all the more difficult to hear His voice or receive His comfort.

We finished our first year of church planting under a tent in a muddy pit with thirty-one waterlogged people. When we got home that afternoon, Kyle said, "It feels like we're starting over." We had been asked to leave our meeting place the previous Friday, we didn't have a new one lined up (hence the tent), we barely had a core group, and we were physically exhausted and emotionally beaten down. We—the fearless leaders—were full of fear and doubt. Privately, I questioned God and His ways. *Lord, we put in the hard work during that difficult first year. Where is the dynamic growth?* I wanted to coast into the second year after the sprint of the first. I was too tired and unprepared to run the distance marathon that church planting requires.

I found myself at a crossroads.

God allowed the difficulty of church planting to sift me, to bring the issues of my heart to the surface. I realized that if I didn't address these things, my marriage, my family, and my own heart were in danger. God was refining me, cleaning me out, and teaching me dependence rather than self-reliance. I could continue my attempts at controlling and relying on myself, or I could submit myself in dependence on Him.

I chose to submit. I found myself agreeing with Peter when he spoke

> We are to diligently maintain a tender soil for God's love and purposes to grow.

to Jesus: "Lord, to whom shall we go? You have the words of eternal life" (John 6:68). I chose to trust Him with my heart and let Him do—through church planting—the work He needed to do in me.

Perhaps you can relate to my struggle.

As church planting wives, we love the Lord and long to be obedient to His calling on our lives, but feelings of loneliness, resentment, discouragement, or exhaustion tempt our hearts to wander from Him. The temptations are subtle, but real: to turn to others, to turn away from the calling because it's difficult and demanding, to distance ourselves from our husbands out of resentment, to feed our children a faint distaste for the church and for God, to believe that our successes in church planting belong to us, to live off of our previous sacrifices and refuse to sacrifice more of ourselves to God. The temptation is to self-seeking our own agenda, clamoring to have our needs met, self-promotion, and selfish ambition. As we seek these things, we become a statistic: burned out, isolated, depressed, and—sometimes—resigned.

It's no wonder that the Bible entreats us to guard our hearts. Proverbs 4:23 (NIV) says, "Above all else, guard your heart, for it is the wellspring of life." The literal interpretation reads, "Above all guarding, guard your heart." We are to guard our hearts more than our children, more than our marriage, more than our reputation, more than our home, more than our schedule, and more than our church. As Matthew Henry says,

> We must keep a watchful eye and a strict hand upon all the motions of the inward man. . . . We must maintain a holy jealousy of ourselves, and set a strict guard . . . upon all the avenues of the soul.[1]

In other words, we are to diligently maintain a tender soil for God's love and purposes to grow, to continually pull out weeds of self-focus, and to allow God to produce fruit in and through us.

This is, in essence, the charge of a church planting wife.

State of the Heart

At Christmas, I make caramelized popcorn as a gift for friends and neighbors. In order to perfect the caramel coating, the mixture must boil for a very specified amount of time at extreme heat. While it's boiling, I have to stir constantly, watching for the liquid to turn the caramel color that will let me know it's ready. Then I must immediately remove it from heat and coat the popcorn before the mixture hardens. I have learned from experience that without my constant diligence and hovering presence, the popcorn will be ruined because it hardens too quickly.

The same hardening process occurs in our hearts when we aren't diligent in watching over them. The pressures, the burdens, and the work of church planting press in on us daily. We need the Holy Spirit's constant help to remain available and moldable before God. Without our submission to the Spirit on a daily basis, it is impossible to have a soft heart and to serve Him as He has called us to. Without that submission, we invite temptation and distraction to draw us away to emotional places and wrong thoughts that harden our hearts. Proverbs 28:14 (NIV) says, "Blessed is the man who always fears the Lord, but he who hardens his heart falls into trouble."

Unfortunately, brittle hearts don't just shatter—they also scatter. If we aren't diligent with our hearts, we will have a negative effect on those close to us.

When I was young, my grandparents took me to Yellowstone National Park, which is famous for Old Faithful, a geyser that gushes on a regular timetable. We stood with the crowd and watched thousands of gallons of boiling water shoot up hundreds of feet into the air from underneath the earth's surface. When I think of the heart, I think of Old Faithful. What goes on below the surface, even things that we try to hide from God and from others, will eventually come spewing out. If we are cultivating a joyful, obedient heart and submitting to the Spirit, good works and good fruit will sprout from our heart's tender soil. But if we do not deal with resentment, bitterness, or rebelliousness, we will spew ugliness all over our husbands, children, and churches and hinder the work of the Spirit in and through us.

As He did with me, God disciplines the one whose lips speak His name while her heart remains far away, or the one who cultivates her own reputation, or the one who goes through the motions of ministry but does not serve from love. If our hearts are far from Him, we will have no ministry and in fact may hinder the work of the gospel in our families and in the lives of those we serve.

However, the Lord renews the one with the contrite and humble heart (Isaiah 57:15). We must continually examine ourselves, asking God to make us tender soil for the seeds through which He grows gospel fruit: "But the seed on good soil stands for those with a noble and good heart, who hear the word, retain it, and by persevering produce a crop" (Luke 8:15 NIV).

The state of my heart determines my ministry and influence. It also determines my attitude and motivations behind what I do. When my heart is His, He empowers me to fulfill this calling. I am able to joyfully die to myself rather than complain about what sacrifices are required of me. I am able to love people rather than grow irritated with their constant needs. I am able to pray for my husband and seek to serve him rather than fight for his attention and time.

> We often feel pressure to say and do all the right things, to be perfect in our service to our husbands, churches, and communities.

As church planting wives, we often feel pressure to say and do all the right things, to be perfect in our service to our husbands, churches, and communities. But God doesn't care to see us play the role of perfect church planting wives, He is not making a checklist of our activities or ministries to evaluate our performance, nor is He making judgments based upon our emotions or circumstances. He is looking at our hearts, not as a gruff man standing at a distance with his arms crossed and face scowled but as a Lover pursuing us with affection. He searches, tests, and weighs our hearts:

Every way of a man is right in his own eyes, but the Lord weighs the heart. (Proverbs 21:2 ESV)

But you, O Lord, know me; you see me, and test my heart toward you. (Jeremiah 12:3 ESV)

What is He searching for?

For the eyes of the Lord range throughout the earth to strengthen those **whose hearts are fully committed to him**. (2 Chronicles 16:9 NIV)

He looks for those whose hearts are undivided, who see the value of His love and His ways. He searches beyond our actions to determine if our hearts are willingly submitted to Him. He weighs our availability to Him: Are we gladly receiving His loving leadership? Are we soft and moldable in His hands? Do we trust Him? He knows our devotions, our intentions, and our motivations.

And when He finds a wholehearted church planting wife who is willing to say, "I need Your help. I am fully Yours," He delights in her. He strengthens and protects her like a loving Father watches over His child. He tends to her heart—pruning, prodding, comforting, and leading. He offers her restful peace in the midst of the work of church planting. Strength, protection, love, comfort, leadership, peace—as church planting wives, aren't those *just* the things we crave and need?

When God searches your heart, what does He see? Is it tender and pliable, purposefully set in the hands of the Father? Or is it hard and resentful, turned away from the One who loves you most? This is of utmost importance because, although your husband is out front, you are just as vital to the mission.

Your heart is vital to the mission.

As you give God your heart, He will give you His. God's heart for you is that church planting be the soil in which you grow in Christlikeness. With His heart as your own, your role and the challenges of church planting become opportunities for growth and ministry, and church planting becomes an exciting adventure of radical faith. With your heart in His hands, you will recognize your opportunity and privilege of being a part of a new work from the ground up, to see and be a part of God changing lives, to engage people with love, to go outside the church walls and meet the needs of your community, and to watch God do the miraculous work of building a church.

If our hearts are His, it's a pretty great life.

Going forward, then, let this be our prayer as we allow the Lord to search and test our hearts:

Create in me a pure heart, O God,
> and renew a steadfast spirit within me.
Do not cast me from your presence or
> remove your Holy Spirit from me.
Restore to me the joy of your salvation and
> grant me a willing spirit, to sustain me.
Then I will teach transgressors your ways,
> and sinners will turn back to you. (Psalm 51:10–13 NIV)

Cultivating Your Heart

Ask yourself these questions. Which are the most difficult to say yes to right now?

Am I willing . . .

> to accept the trials and discouragement for His sake?
> to follow Him wherever He leads?
> to lay aside fear and anxiety?
> to support my husband's calling?
> to give up my life to follow Christ?
> to trust Him with my whole heart?

Take some moments to meditate on these Scriptures from the chapter, and jot down others that are meaningful to you.

Above all else, guard your heart, for it is the wellspring of life. (Proverbs 4:23 NIV)

But you, O Lord, know me; you see me, and test my heart toward you. (Jeremiah 12:3 ESV)

But the seed on good soil stands for those with a noble and good heart, who hear the word, retain it, and by persevering produce a crop. (Luke 8:15 NIV)

For thus says the High and Lofty One
Who inhabits eternity, whose name *is* Holy:
"I dwell in the high and holy place,
With him who has a contrite and humble spirit,
To revive the spirit of the humble,
And to revive the heart of the contrite ones." (Isaiah 57:15)

Your experience in church planting will inevitably be determined by the condition of your heart. Thankfully, if you surrender to our good and loving God, He will do the primary work of guarding and cultivating your heart. After all, your heart is what He wants most from you.

CHAPTER TWO

the Dependent Heart

THE CHURCH PLANTING WIFE'S JOB DESCRIPTION

As we prepared to church plant, my consistent prayer was, "Lord, show me my role in this." Being a teensy-weensy bit Type A, I preferred He give me a job description of sorts, neatly typed in bullet points under the heading "How to Be a Perfect Church Planter's Wife." I wanted some idea of what I'd be doing and what would be required of me, but He only spoke in generalities. *Follow Me. Serve your family. Love people.*

Yes, Lord, but what do I *do?*

A God-Fearing Ken and Barbie

Hoping for more specifics, I pictured well-known church planting wives sitting serenely in the front row of a warehouse/renovated grocery store/church, attentive to their husbands as they preached to large, hipster crowds. The women in my mind appeared quiet. Adored. *Perfect.*

I do this sometimes, this panicked flailing, this grasping for clarity, this desperate need to know what I'm doing. When life changes, my fleshly response is usually to attempt reining in my uncertainties.

27

When my husband took his first ministry position as a college pastor in an established church, then too, I tried formulating a precise ministry wife job description for myself. I asked the Lord some of the same frantic questions, really wanting to get it right.

The ideas I generated were based on Mrs. Fenton, the pastor's wife at the church I attended growing up. As a teenager, I sat with the rest of the youth group in the first rows of the sanctuary week after week, which gave me a perfect view of her. Every Sunday, Mrs. Fenton sat to the left of us near the aisle where her pastor-husband retrieved her during the closing hymn, escorting her to the back doors so they could greet the congregation as they left. I noticed how he approached her seat, how he smiled as she took his offered hand, and how, like a God-fearing Ken and Barbie, they walked down the aisle together. After the service, as I exited with my family, I anticipated their handshakes with nervous excitement, wondering if they would give me special attention. Being spiritual giants, it seemed that they saw straight into my soul.

I counted it a great privilege to be friends with the Fentons' daughter, which gave me access to a wonderful family and home. I was acutely aware of Mrs. Fenton anytime she entered a room, taking note of her words, her appearance, and how she related to her husband and children. Without fail, she was warm, loving, inviting, and hospitable, just like she was at church when she greeted everyone by name while happily moving from group to group. In my esteem, she and her family were ideal.

When Kyle and I began in ministry, naturally I wanted to be just like Mrs. Fenton. But as I attempted to piece together a job description for myself based on what she had done, I quickly realized that despite my careful observance of her, I had no recollection of what she actually did beyond being a decoration on her husband's arm, a greeter, or a picture of perfection, always seen but rarely heard. Typical of most teenagers, I hadn't considered Mrs. Fenton as a real person with imperfections, struggles, or weaknesses. I also hadn't

> God taught me that I didn't need to be the perfect ministry wife or play some role I had conjured up for myself.

measured how hard she worked while serving her husband, children, and the members of our church. Even though I had been in her home countless times, I didn't know what occurred beyond "the role."

I still, however, tried imitating her, or at least what she represented. I played the role of the model minister's wife, attempting to earn the respect of others, striving to please people and meet all their expectations. I copied women I admired but who were gifted differently than I was. Burdened with a self-imposed list of "shoulds" and "should nots," I attempted to prove my worth to God, to others, and especially to myself.

I felt like a failure, but was unable to extract myself from the merry-go-round of performance.

Through time, God changed my heart. He taught me that I didn't need to be the perfect ministry wife or play some role I had conjured up for myself. Instead, like anyone else, I was to walk in an intimate and dependent relationship with Him. Out of the overflow of that relationship, He would develop my ministry. Through this simple yet profound lesson, He removed the weight of the "shoulds" from my back.

The Lord brought all this to mind as I prayerfully prepared for church planting, as I frantically sought clarification for my role. He simply whispered grace and freedom over me, reiterating what He had already said: *Follow Me. Serve your family. Love people.*

Yes, Lord, but what do I *do?*

What *Does* She Do?

What *does* a church planting wife do?

Often, when answering this question to ourselves or to others, we tend to talk about our "role" in the plant. I don't like that word because it implies an aspect of activity, duty, and expectations. If being a church planting wife is a role—something we do—then it is about our performance. We may begin feeling like an actor who must respond to direction or dutifully speak scripted lines. Before long, we find ourselves playing the stereotype—what we think a church planting wife does—and our hearts, with our gifts and passions, get buried underneath the so-called role. Sometimes, because we are trying to fulfill some standard we have set for ourselves or we believe others have for us, we even lose the ability to hear the Lord or authentically fulfill this calling He's given us.

When actors prepare for a role, they search for their character's motivation. The motivations for the role of the Perfect Church Planting Wife are often internal "shoulds" that result in "good" activities.

A *church planting wife should reach out to unbelievers, so I will invite the neighbors over for dinner.*

A *church planting wife should help her husband in the plant, so I will run the kids' ministry even though I'm gifted elsewhere.*

A *church planting wife should be accessible to women in the church, so I will accept every invitation.*

If we live this way—dedicated to the "should," performing for others and for God, trying to meet some false standard—it does a number on our hearts, causing a wild vacillation between pride and self-condemnation. We begin needing the role in order to feel like we're doing the right things, that we're doing enough, that *we're enough*. We need validation and confirmation. We train ourselves to act, speak, and live in such a way to garner our audience's approval. When we receive it, we relish the glory, the attention, and the respect. But when the audience grows quiet or critical, we despair about what we are doing wrong, complain that we're unappreciated, and commit to earning their favor once again.

> A good church planting wife is one who lives and leads out of her relationship with God.

Reject the Role, Accept the Calling

A good church planting wife, one who has an impact on her city, is one who rejects the notion that she plays a prescribed role. Instead, she knows her position as the wife of a pastor and church planter is a calling. She believes wholeheartedly that this mission to church plant is just as much hers as it is her husband's, and she actively seeks to fulfill that calling on her life. She believes with certainty that God has a certain purpose for her family, ministry, and good works within her community, a purpose that she alone can satisfy. Because of her certainty in her calling, because she declines to perform for an audience's approval, and because her eyes are fixed on Christ alone, she is compelled outward to serve and lead for the glory of God. As He fixes her priorities, she uses her gifts and relies on His power to accomplish all that He gives her to accomplish.

Because of this, there is no job description or checklist for how to be a church planting wife. Nor should there be. A good church planting wife is one who lives and leads out of her relationship with God. Oswald Chambers says, "Your duty in service and ministry is to make sure there is nothing between Jesus and yourself."[2] Colossians 1:10 seems to sum it up: ". . . walk worthy of the Lord, fully pleasing Him, being fruitful in every good work and increasing in the knowledge of God." If the church planting wife is increasing in her knowledge of God, she *will* be fruitful in every good work and she will have plenty of opportunity for good works as she leads ministries, cares for her husband and children, prints bulletins, hosts church events in her home, engages her community, sets up chairs, and does the host of things church planting wives may be called to do.

All along, however, she allows Christ to fix her priorities, not anyone or anything else, including herself.

I have discovered that as I allow God to fix my priorities, He takes me back to our original interchange at our transition points in ministry, the times when I've freaked out with bullet pointed lists and lofty ideals regarding all I should be accomplishing. *Follow Me. Serve your family. Love others.* He speaks gentle, simple words that remind me it is not as difficult as I make it out to be. My priorities are unchanging and fixed in a certain order for this season of life: be a disciple of Christ, love and help my husband, love and train my children, serve in our church in specific ways, and engage my community through work and play. How those priorities flesh out may change on the daily or seasonal calendar and will certainly create a full schedule that requires my diligence and consistency, but having them front and center in my heart helps me mark my calling like a bull's-eye on a target.

My friend Aimee commented once that I lead a very structured life. I hadn't thought of it that way before, but she was right. I have found that I must proactively structure and plan my days in order to fulfill my calling. I am a disciple first, so God gets my early mornings. I am a wife second, so I must protect and plan evenings, weekends, and special retreats for Kyle and me to connect and rest. I am a mom third, which means my children have my undivided attention during their nonschool hours. Finally, I maintain certain time slots each week that I can meet with other women or prepare for ministry events, as well as give some evenings to hospitality or community groups.

When I get overwhelmed, sidetracked, or am missing the mark of my calling, I've discovered it's because *I'm* adding or changing the priority list without consulting with the Lord, or I'm doing things because I think it's what other people expect from me.

The ability to reject ministry as a dutiful role, embrace it as our calling, and maintain our God-given priorities happens only through our utter dependence on the Lord.

> For perhaps the very first time, I had an opportunity to believe God and to live in utter dependence on Him.

At the beginning, church planting is an adrenaline rush of fear and faith. We resolve to depend on Jesus, because our need for Him is so clear, but remaining dependent is difficult because everything in life hangs in the balance.

Will the church make it?
What happens if it doesn't?
Are we completely insane? Can God be trusted?
What is our plan B?
Should we have a plan B?

In the beginning, Kyle and I spent many sleepless nights trying to concretely answer those questions, but in the end, our choices were either faith or flailing despair. Sadly, I often chose despair.

Looking back, I realize that those days of despair were really withdrawals. All of my life, I had depended on myself, controlled circumstances (or at least tried), and avoided any ministry outside what

I was comfortable with. I also had always had a people buffer: people to lead, disciple, encourage me, or validate my ministry. But like a soul tsunami, church planting completely and swiftly wiped out all my self-made security. For perhaps the very first time, I had an opportunity to believe God and to live in utter dependence on Him.

Slowly, the withdrawals from self-sustenance became less and less and I learned needy, childlike dependence. I learned to embrace the feeling of vulnerability, knowing that I am forced to trust God in that position. I learned to step out from behind the Perfect Church Planter's Wife role and her script and be who God intended for me to be in this work.

There still aren't any guarantees that things will work out how I think they should or how I want them to. Something could go wrong, and then what?

No matter who you are or what kind of church planting work you're doing or what is going on with your church, you will face the decision daily: faith or fear? dependence or independence? In fact, those are questions for all believers seeking to live a life of faith, church planting or not. Everything hangs in the balance and things feel a little wobbly all the time.

But that is where we meet Christ. He's not in our independence and control and plan Bs. In all the uncertainty and instability of church planting, we don't have to despair for He holds all things together. Rather than expending our energy attempting to control life, rather than trying to fulfill some false standard of perfection, we must instead cultivate a dependent heart.

The Sower and the Grower

Cultivating a dependent heart begins with an understanding of who it is we are depending on and what we're depending on Him for. Considering that we are church planting wives, I find it interesting that Scripture describes dependence on God, especially regarding fruitful ministry, in gardening terms. Paul called himself a sower and God the grower: "I planted, Apollos watered, but God gave the increase. So then neither he who plants is anything, nor he who waters, but God who gives the increase" (1 Corinthians 3:6–7).

Our friends Phil and Amy recently purchased acres of land in the hills outside our city. They dubbed their land Spring Forth Farm, dreaming of the day its trees overflow with fruit, and when the farm is fully functioning. So far, they have spent the majority of their time and backbreaking labor on preparing the soil to plant trees and clearing land for fencing. When I visited them, they proudly showed me the orchard, rows of saplings standing at attention. Amy informed me that the trees will take several years to mature enough to bear fruit and that there is no guarantee that they will stay healthy enough to actually do so.

> We both work extremely hard alongside our husbands at what God has given us to do, but at the end of the day, neither of us has control over the outcome.

Amy and I marvel at how similar our experiences are as a farmer's wife and a church planter's wife. In the past year, we have both turned over soil, prepared it for planting, poked seeds and saplings in the ground, and prayed earnestly while watching for signs of life. We are both sowers, but neither of us has the ability to make our seeds take root and grow. We both work extremely hard alongside our husbands at what God has given us to do, but at the end of the day, neither of us has control over the outcome. Amy and Phil can't produce crops through effort alone. Truly, each harvest is a gift of grace. The same can be said for the church planter and his wife—the harvest doesn't come from hard work alone; it is a work of the Holy Spirit. As the farmer prays for the proper amount of sunshine and rain, so the church planter trusts God for an environment conducive for spiritual growth.

At times, this has scared me at a very deep heart level. *You mean I can serve the Lord in the church by reaching out to my community, discipling new believers, and having people in my home, but there is no guarantee the church will actually succeed?* The only consolation keeping me from complete panic at that thought is knowing that we don't work alone. We are the sowers, planting meager seeds in the ground, but God is the grower. By the leading of the Holy Spirit, He directs our planting and gifts us for the job. He then takes our acts of obedience, carried out in faith, and makes something of them. He does the miraculous, the supernatural, of calling fruit into existence.

In church planting, it's difficult to remember that God is the grower because of the hard work, resources, time, and emotional energy it requires. But the key to our spiritual, emotional, and even physical health is, while acting in obedience through our hard work, we also depend on God to give the increase. If we trust Him that He has called us to plant the church, we can also trust Him that He will do the work of growing what we are planting. We can praise Him when fruit bursts forth and we can praise Him when things don't work out as we hoped, because we know that He is the grower, He will produce fruit as He sees fit, and He is pleased with our faithful sowing. There is peace knowing God always does His job thoroughly. "He who calls you is faithful, who also will do it" (1 Thessalonians 5:24).

The Vine and the Branches

Jesus uses a second gardening word picture to further illustrate our dependent relationship on Him. In John 15:1, 5 (NIV), He says: "I am the true vine, and my Father is the gardener . . . you are the branches. If a man remains in me and I in him, he will bear much fruit; apart from me you can do nothing."

I am not a master gardener, but I know that the branches or leaves of a vine could not live long if they were removed from the source of their nourishment. I also know that the burden of responsibility in agriculture lies with the gardener. Jesus says this is the foundation of all ministry, that as we remain in Him, He tends the vineyard—His church—watering, protecting, and cultivating it so that it will produce a maximum, bountiful yield. Continued production in the vineyard depends on the branch's constant union with the source of fruitfulness. Branches that are severed from the parent stock may produce leaves temporarily, but inevitably they will wither because there is no source of life to sustain them; and they will never bear fruit. Our effectiveness as a believer depends on our receiving the constant flow of life from Christ.[3]

This image of the vine and branches evokes a picture of total dependence. Happily, we are asked to depend on the One who loves us best. "As the Father has loved me, so I have loved you. Now remain in my love" (John 15:9 NIV). In other words, we abandon our lives to One who has our very best interests in mind, who leads perfectly, and who is completely trustworthy. He not only carries the burden of responsibility in our lives, but He also initiates and pursues us in our love relationship with Him.

So often, we incorrectly believe that we are responsible for ministry outcomes: changed hearts, transformed lives, and the movement of God. Because the work is so demanding, this belief is especially tempting to church planters and their wives. We expend our best efforts in order for the church to take root, survive, and grow. We erroneously believe that the amount of work we do *determines* the outcome. *If* we plan an outreach event, *then* our church will grow. *If* we have a new family over for dinner, *then* they will join our church. *If* we start a new moms' Bible study in our neighborhood, *then* many will come and be saved. Both the *ifs* and the *thens* become our responsibilities.

> We take the vending machine approach— we insert an activity or program and expect a fully functioning church to pop out.

I didn't even realize I believed this fallacy of ministry until we started church planting. In our prior, established church, I enjoyed results from teaching and discipling college women. Surely, I thought, my experience and skills, combined with my husband's giftedness, would help us achieve similar success in church planting.

But when we arrived in our new city and invited everyone we met to our first church gathering, there was not a stampede to our door. It didn't matter to anyone that I was a pastor's wife or that we were here, like Superman stepping out of the phone booth, to save the city. We thought our passion and hard work would produce immediate results, but we were wrong. We didn't have the ability to change hearts, and clinging to that belief only produced feelings of failure. In fact, we discovered that He might use a simple interaction with our neighbor to draw many people to Himself while using a community-wide outreach event to do very little spiritually. Through the discouragement of the first year, God continually revealed the pride behind my belief that I could produce spiritual fruit apart from Him.

If ministry depends on us, it becomes an equation, a formula, or a puzzle to piece together; the Spirit of God is removed entirely. We take His place, casting ourselves in the role of God, thinking we can put in enough effort to squeeze spiritual fruit from a planted seed. If that belief plays out, church planting and, really, the entire Christian life becomes a works-based system, devoid of faith. As a result of our self-sufficiency, we vacillate between extreme self-condemnation and pride. We wonder when we have done "enough" work. We revel in success because it has obviously resulted from our skills, our personalities, and our efforts. There is no true peace or joy in ministry in this system because it requires constant plate spinning—nothing can fall and new plates need to go up at shorter and shorter intervals.

How much is enough? What happens when numerical or spiritual growth plateaus despite our best intentions or efforts? What happens when other church plants grow faster than ours or when our husbands are criticized? God's loving whispers, leading and guiding us, are drowned out by the demands of our own checklist and the critical human voices.

When we believe that we're responsible for producing results, we don't trust God to be God. We can't rest because no amount of work is ever enough. We can't rejoice when God blesses others. We can't handle criticism. We scream and cry at our husbands because we are burned out and resentful. We neglect our children and our homes for the sake of our reputations in ministry. We don't have eyes to see the fruit God is bringing forth and what we do see isn't good enough. The joy of ministry is completely lost.

Then, as we hold our closed fists up toward heaven, we wonder why God isn't doing His gardening job. Can't He see that we're working so hard?

However, as we increasingly recognize and acknowledge God as gardener and grower, we learn to depend on Him. A dependent heart is one that says *I need, therefore I follow. I need, but I will not try to control or strive. I trust that You will take care of me. I trust that You will lead me and bear fruit from my ministry.* In dependence, our lives come to rest at the feet of Christ where, as we abide there, He continually persists in the work of ministry in our hearts, our homes, and our churches.

Unlimited Supply

Knowing who God is helps us to depend on Him, but knowing that the supply of help He gives is unlimited is just as vital.

I am a mom to three growing boys. Aside from my persistent battle with poorly aimed pee in the bathroom and their constant running (mostly into each other), wrestling, and light saber fights, the major distinction of mothering boys is supplying their ravenous bellies with food.

All day long, it seems, I am pestered for food and/or drink. Just after a meal is completed, but just before I am finished cleaning up in the kitchen, there is a boy at my side asking for a snack (or a complete second meal). I dream of installing a machine in my kitchen that dispenses a fully cooked meal with one press of a button. At some point, in between making the second sandwich and tearing off the third banana from the bunch, I put my foot down: "Kitchen's closed! Food rationing begins! Come back at breakfast!" I'm like a circus lion tamer trapped in a cage with hungry, prowling animals, fending them off with a kitchen stool.

With boys and food, it is constant demand, but limited supply.

But it's not just with boys and it's not just with food. Is there any area of life not characterized by constant demand and limited supply? Parenting, housework, marriage, work, relationships, *certainly church planting*—these demand our attention, time, effort, patience, love, persistence, and commitment. In the end, however, we can only give so much. According to our human limits, as we give out to others, our supplies must be replenished. If they are not replenished, we become like a lion tamer fending off weariness, discouragement, dryness, or emptiness. Or perhaps anger, bitterness, or feelings of being unloved or alone.

Where can we replenish our supplies so that we might give to others? Where do we turn when so much is demanded of us, yet so little is given in return? Who will care for us?

The Lord will, for He *never* grows weary of demands, *never* needs a break, *never* sleeps, *never* takes time off.

This is how we thrive.

This is how we church plant.

We go to the Source, tell Him our needs, fill up on Him, let Him live in us, and then rise up, empowered to meet the demands of life.

He never says, "Kitchen's closed. Come back tomorrow," for His supply is unlimited and freely, joyfully given.

Cultivating Dependency

We recognize that God is the grower, the gardener, and our limitless source of help, so just how do we practice our dependency on Him in daily life? In the midst of laundry, lunch boxes, and leading, what does it mean to remain in Christ?

I have a vivid memory of youth camp during my senior year in high school when, during a late-night debriefing of the day's events, I said, "I want to live life in such a way that I fall into bed each night exhausted from serving the Lord."

I'm not sure about the exact wording I used to convey my thoughts, but I specifically remember using the word "exhausted."

My youth minister nodded solemnly, but I'm sure on the inside he was laughing hysterically. A teenager knows little about exhaustion, unless it's the morning after a slumber party. What did I know then about the exhaustion that comes from middle-of-the-night feedings or chasing toddlers or the demands of ministry? Nothing, of course. But I said it. And I think I remember it so vividly because it was Spirit-inspired. He was drawing me, preparing me for what was to come.

Through church planting, I have learned dependence mostly through exhaustion.

When I'm weary, I recognize my very limited supply in the face of great demand. I have not been able to get the searing mental image out of my head of my teenage self spouting my desire to be exhausted for the Lord. *Exhaustion*, He reminds me, *is not always a bad thing.* As Oswald Chambers puts it,

Exhaustion means that the vital forces are worn right out. Spiritual exhaustion never comes through sin but only through service, and whether or not you are exhausted will depend upon where you get your supplies. Jesus said to Peter—"Feed My sheep," but He gave him nothing to feed them with. The process of being made broken bread and poured out wine means that you have to be the nourishment for other souls until they learn to feed on God. They must drain you to the dregs. Be careful that you get your supply, or before long you will be utterly exhausted. Before other souls learn to draw on the life of the Lord Jesus direct, they have to draw on it through you; you have to be literally "sucked," until they learn to take their nourishment from God. We owe it to God to be our best for His lambs and His sheep as well as for Himself.

Has the way in which you have been serving God betrayed you into exhaustion? If so, then rally your affections. Where did you start the service from? From your own sympathy or from the basis of the Redemption of Jesus Christ? Continually go back to the foundation of your affections and recollect where the source of power is. You have no right to say—"O Lord, I am so exhausted." He saved and sanctified you in order to exhaust you. Be exhausted for God, but remember that your supply comes from Him. "All my fresh springs shall be in Thee."[4]

Most of the time, I am not that bold teenager eager to fall in bed, exhausted from serving my Lord. Instead, I avoid exhaustion at all costs. I wrongly believe that church planting should be comfortable and easy, not about self-death and pouring out. *It shouldn't be this hard,* I tell myself. *I shouldn't feel so exhausted.* But that is usually because I have not returned to Him for my supply.

We will never develop a dependent heart unless we consistently give of ourselves to others and then return to the source of our supply. Perhaps it seems contradictory to say that God does the fruit bearing in and through us, but that we must also practice spiritual disciplines. Why, with grace and with the Holy Spirit doing the work in our lives, do we need to consistently spend time with the Lord through Bible reading and prayer?

Back to the Basics

When we spend time with God, we are making ourselves available to Him. We're cultivating dependence, opening the door to receive, and fueling up to give. Oh, how we need these things! We read the Bible in order to hear and follow the leading of the Holy Spirit. We're not trying to conjure up an experience or check an obligation off our Perfect Church Planting Wife to-do list. Instead, we're making ourselves available and letting God be God, like the psalmist, who said: "When You said, 'Seek My face,' my heart said to You, 'Your face, Lord, I will seek'" (Psalm 27:8). As we receive truth from Scripture or experience the Holy Spirit impressing something on our heart, we can then respond in obedience. We breathe in, we breathe out.

That is why consistency is important. The more we make ourselves available, the more opportunities He has to speak to us and the more we know Him. We also have the opportunity to lay our cares before Him, vocalizing our dependence on Him. When we lack motivation, energy, and love for people, time with God is an opportunity to remember why we're doing this work, to cast our cares on Him, to receive encouragement and comfort, and to be reminded that He is trustworthy.

Dependence does not develop from obligatory quiet times but from an intimate relationship and daily reliance on God. It is not something a Perfect Church Planting Wife checks off her list; it is a necessity for survival. If we don't cultivate dependence on God by spending time with Him, we will certainly be tempted to take on responsibilities that aren't ours, experience burnout, and look to people to meet our heart's needs.

Without dependence, we start going through the motions and playing the role.

Dependence on the Lord qualifies us for ministry. If we are going to be effective, a strong sense of our need must always remain. We don't often like this vulnerable position where we lack control, where the outcome is uncertain, or where things might turn out much different than we imagined. Even in our dependence, we won't know that the church will have a reliable worship leader by a certain time or that someone will instantly step forward to lead the children's ministry. But our dependence on the Lord solidifies our intimacy with Him, and it assures that we will grow and bear fruit. Depending on Him means that we have everything we need, and we are everything He wants us to be.

In all my attempts at forming a job description for myself, God has continually spoken grace over me: *Follow Me. Serve your family. Love people.* As much as I panic and attempt a bullet point to-do list, He always brings me back to dependence:

Child, abide in Me. As a church planting wife, dependence is what you do.

Cultivating Your Heart

Do you identify with these statements from this chapter: "Where do we turn when so much is demanded of us, yet so little is given in return? Who will care for us?" In what ways?

God's priorities for you are to be a disciple, a loving wife, a faithful mother (if you have children), and then to engage in your church and community. Are your priorities in order? Are you making them more complex by adding in your own agenda or by allowing others to set your priorities?

What does it mean to you to "remain in Christ"? Can you spot areas in which you have stepped out of your dependence on Him?

When have you proven that He is reliable? Take a few moments and review times when you've seen His hand on your situation and renew your dependence on Him for current ones.

Joshua 4:1–7; 19–24; 1 Chronicles 16:8–12; Psalms 103:1–5; 105:1–5; 143

As a church planting wife, your one job is to remain in Christ and, in the conversation you have together, listen for His love, conviction, and direction. When He says *go*, it's your job to go. When He says *wait*, it's your job to wait. When He says *no*, it's your job to obey. When He convicts, it's your job to repent and allow Him to cleanse your heart. In other words, your job is to abide.

As your heart is tuned to Him, rather than to yourself, He will meet your needs and tune your heart to those He wants you to serve. As you depend on Him, seek Him, read His Word, and listen to Him, He will tell you by His Spirit what He wants you to do. The checklist is thrown out the window; you don't have to worry about doing or being enough because He has made you enough. His leading and His love are perfect.

The Lord *never* grows weary of demands, *never* needs a break, *never* sleeps, *never* takes time off.

The Lord's love, grace, mercy, and patience are *endless*.

The Lord says we can cast *all* of our cares on Him.

The Lord is an *endless* supply on whom we can ravenously feast.

The Lord *never* leaves us to fend for ourselves.

How can you practice depending on Him?

Interview with

Lauren
Chandler

Lauren's husband, Matt, is the pastor of The Village Church in Flower Mound, Texas. They replanted the church in 2002, and since then, the church has grown from sixty to a multisite church reaching thousands of people. Lauren and Matt are the parents of three children.

What advice would you give to church planting wives who are in the beginning stages of church planting?

Remember that your first ministry is in your home: to your husband and, if applicable, to your children. No matter what demands are placed on you because of the church, do not attend to them at the expense of your home. Also, keep careful watch over your own heart and soul. If needed, see a professional, biblical counselor. There is no shame in that. There was a season early in our life at The Village where I desperately needed that kind of help. I probably could have seen the counselor sooner but fell into the trap of thinking I'd just try harder: read my Bible more faithfully, pray more earnestly, and just be less self-centered. Of course, that never worked because I was more set on perfecting the flesh than dealing with the deep roots of pride in my heart.

In those first two years, what were the most difficult aspects of (re) planting for you and how did you work through those struggles?

When we came, I was eight months pregnant with our first child. It's hard to know if the "growing pains" I experienced were as a result of becoming a pastor's wife and replanting a church or of becoming a mother. Motherhood rocked me. I no longer had the "luxury" of being self-focused. On the flip side, motherhood protected me from the unfair demands and expectations that sometimes come with planting/replanting. Matt did a great job protecting me too. I was given the chance to speak in front of the core congregation (about sixty) and state my intention of putting my home first. If ministry poured from that, I would pursue it. In other words, I kept first things first and let others who were in a more appropriate season of life carry the weight of ministry. I didn't have the demand or expectation of leading worship, teaching Sunday school, organizing the children's ministry or women's ministry, etc. I know that is not everyone else's experience. Sometimes you just have to do what is necessary. However, if it comes at the expense of your home and the health of your soul (as long as your heart is rooted in the Lord and not simply subversive), have a conversation with your husband. Join together in asking the Lord to fill spots that you currently fill at the expense of your home.

How are you a helpmate to your husband?

I try to make home a safe place for Matt. After a full day at the office, in meetings, handling problems that my brain can hardly imagine or heart can hardly take, the last thing he wants to come home to is a needy wife who is grilling him about how he is running the church. I have learned this the hard way. Even sincere questions with no malicious intent about the church at the wrong time are devastating to your intimacy with your husband. At the right time, it can be life giving. I want to know what's going on and how I can pray for Matt in leading the church. I want to be the iron sharpening iron. But I need the Spirit's wisdom in determining the right time. Also, I don't look to Matt to satisfy my need for significance and value. Yes, he does make me feel significant and valuable but the weight of that does not fall entirely on him. Instead, it falls on the Father and understanding His love for me because of Christ.

I try to be a friend to Matt. I love just being with him. We've had pillow fights. We've been goofy together. We watch "guy" movies (though I secretly like most of them) together. I listen when he tells me obscure facts about football.

I try to be responsive to his approach. The last thing he wants is to be rejected by me. I want to be the most responsive to his advances. It pleases God. It pleases Matt. And, in the end, even when I may not be "in the mood," it pleases me.

With being such an influential couple and in a demanding ministry role, how do you protect against isolation and loneliness? How do you maintain community, openness, and connection with others?

I am blessed to have a group of about ten women at The Village with whom I've walked for almost five years. Some are on staff, some are staff wives, and others are covenant members. We have walked through more than I could ever imagine in those five years. It has been a tremendous blessing and one of the most intense times of growth in my walk with the Lord. I do not lead the group. Our leader is in her forties and has more ministry experience, and I love and respect her. I know that this is rare to have especially as a lead pastor's wife. I am grateful for it.

Also, I was involved—as a participant first and then a leader—in our Recovery ministry for a couple of years. There was definitely a lot of openness and connecting with others there. Honestly, it was what I needed. I needed to stop pretending I had it all together. That's a real danger in being a wife of a pastor. We easily buy into the lie that we have to look like we've got it all together while we're dying inside. If you don't start walking in openness about your sin, you eventually start believing you do have it all together and that's when you can end up ruining your marriage and your ministry and your own soul.

How do you protect your marriage and family from the demands of ministry?

Matt, his assistant, a couple of elders, and I meet together about twice a year to look at Matt's schedule and outside speaking engagements. If it looks like an exceptionally busy week is ahead for us, we intentionally shut down the social calendar (or make it home-based) the week before.

Concerning the demands of living as a family on "display," we strive to live with integrity. We don't want to come off to others as something we are not at home. This means we strive to have family devotions and not miss what's going on in the hearts of our kids or each other. We are by no means perfect, and our children see that the most. We say "sorry" and "forgive me" and "I was wrong" a LOT. We do not want to forget that our first ministry is to our children. A wise, godly woman reminded me that there's a reason the Lord placed them with us, and so do not buy into the idea that we can't treat them preferentially in ministry. I want them to be the most important converts to me. I want to be more concerned with mentoring them than mentoring a million "influential" young women.

How do you resist being pulled by the expectations of others?

This may sound crazy, but I think the Lord has protected me from knowing most of the expectations of others on me. I struggle with the fear of man so any expectations I do sense, I use as an opportunity to press into the Lord and operate in the fear of Him and not of them. I also want to make sure it isn't the Lord nudging me to step out in something. I just go to Him and to Matt and ask for wisdom. Being Matt's wife has given me compassion and mercy toward people of influence who have people vying for their attention and time constantly. I want to be gracious and not set expectations that are unfair on them because I wouldn't want them placed on me either!

What do you like most about being a pastor's wife?

I love the people of The Village. I love their stories. I love what God is doing in them and through them. I am grateful that we get to see it and be a part of it. My favorite weekends are our baptism weekends. To hear the testimonies of how the Lord is working is overwhelming.

CHAPTER THREE

the Helping Heart

BEING A WISE HELPMATE TO THE CHURCH PLANTER

In 2007, because of Kyle's conversation with other church planters, Kyle and I attended a church planting conference. We went to that conference knowing God wanted change for us, but fully expecting that we would leave able to cross church planting off the list of possibilities. Honestly, at that time, I didn't even have a good understanding of what church planting actually entails. Less than a year later, however, Kyle had resigned his ministry position, we had raised both a team and financial support, we had moved across the country, and we had started the church he now pastors.

Because They Described *Him*

This is why: because, through that conference, *I knew* God was calling us to plant a church.

This is how I knew: when the speakers, all experienced church planters, described the kind of man God uses to do this work, they described my husband.

Church planting, they said, is a difficult and unique work. Similar to pastoring an existing church, it must be done by a qualified elder, a man who is able to teach, able to shepherd, able to lead, above reproach, respectable, hospitable. Because of the unique work of church planting, however, the church planter must also possess the gifts of apostleship, leadership, evangelism, and teaching. He must work tirelessly, serve as the only elder until other elders are appointed, and have the ability to pull the church toward God's mission with the strength of an ox.

During the conference, Kyle and I slipped away for conversation. Clearly, we said, God is speaking to us, but what exactly was He saying? Kyle in particular questioned whether or not he possessed the gifts of a church planter.

In our marriage, I have always been the emotional one, the one who wears my feelings on my sleeve. Kyle is the steady one, not prone to fear, insecurities, or discouragement. While I have wanted to please people, he is not afraid to gently confront or make difficult decisions. He is a great leader, one who people eagerly follow and respect. Without a single doubt, I knew he would make a great church planter. It was *me* I was worried about!

His Weary Hands

Over the course of the next nine months, I watched Kyle step out from under the protection of being on a large church staff—a place where he never had to make the final call on a churchwide decision—and take on the responsibility of starting a church from the ground up. There was so much to do: raise support, gather a team, develop a vision for the church, prepare prayer support, move the family, and establish the church structure. Even as we began meeting for Bible study/church in our home in our new city, the tasks were endless: evangelism, prayer, networking, meeting people, and preparing sermons. His work was hard, only surpassed by the weight of responsibility he felt to succeed and to provide for our family.

Because of this weight and the slow growth of our church, I watched my husband grow weary and discouraged. At the end of each day, when we sat on the couch together, tired and emotionally drained, he often looked at me with fear in his eyes. My husband—an innately gifted leader—questioned his abilities and wondered if there would ever actually be people to lead. Clearly, he was not yet in his ministry sweet spot, and he was a little shaken.

Instead of getting scared by the fear in his eyes or the discouragement in his voice, I recognized my opportunity to encourage him. Like Moses, he needed an Aaron to hold his weary hands up during the battle. And I could be his Aaron. I had always needed him to help me navigate ministry's waters, but now, clearly, he needed me.

In the beginning, I had affirmed his calling and, by going along wholeheartedly, taken it as my own. But once we got into the nitty-gritty of church planting life, I discovered that my helping ministry to my husband—a ministry only I could do—would be crucial to his success and well-being. I had a wifely job to do and I wanted to do it well.

All on the Line

Have you considered how this calling affects your husband? What does his life as a church planter look like? What responsibilities and burdens does he carry because of his job?

Your husband has put everything on the line—his ability to provide, the well-being of his family, his reputation, and his faith—to follow God's calling. On a daily basis, he is breaking up spiritually hard ground, preparing the soil, planting seeds, praying for growth, and cultivating fragile crops. The growth, when it comes, arrives as a sapling after much backbreaking toil and, even then, must be carefully maintained as it grows into a mature, fruit-bearing tree. His work involves engaging people on a deep spiritual level, resolving conflict, making difficult decisions, dealing with life–altering issues, counseling, training leaders, correctly handling the Word of God, and bearing the responsibility for the spiritual health of his God-given flock, with little help, appreciation, acknowledgment, or encouragement. In addition, he has a marriage and family to lead and nourish.

> God has called both of you to plant a church: one to lead and the other to help.

He is most likely a strong, capable leader, but he's not immune to discouragement and fear. He needs your support, help, and encouragement. How you view your husband's call and respond to him may be the greatest indicator of his success in church planting.

God has called both of you to plant a church: one to lead and the other to help. To be clear, you are the helper, not the leader. Though you may be a strong, capable leader in your own right, your calling is not to tell your husband what to do or how to run the church. Your calling is to be his helper. The Bible uses the term *helpmate* to describe this unique calling. According to Douglas Wilson, being a helpmate means:

> The man needs the help; the woman needs to help. Marriage was created by God to provide companionship in the labor of dominion. The cultural mandate, the requirement to fill and subdue the earth, is still in force, and a husband cannot fulfill this portion of the task in isolation. He needs a companion suitable for him in the work to which God has called him. He is called to work and must receive help from her. She is called to the work through ministering to him. He is oriented to the task, and she is oriented to him.[5]

I so easily forget this when my husband is busy or away from home, leaving me with household duties and child-rearing responsibilities. I imagine him sitting at a coffee shop, leisurely studying the Bible, laughing with friends over lunch, or being inundated with encouragement and praise. If I'm honest, there have even been times when I have questioned if he's working hard, doing enough to reach people and grow the church, or if he's carefully considering the security and stability of our family. After all, I huff, he dragged me clear across the country, confined me in this ministry lifestyle, and then succumbed to the demanding needs of others.

A "Together" Calling

In reality, Kyle carefully considered his calling before we moved, faithfully followed the Lord's direction, and purposefully leads both our church and our family. He has always worked extremely hard, never slacking or neglecting his responsibilities, even when there was little to show for his efforts.

My response toward my husband, I've discovered, is all a matter of my perspective. If I trust that God has called my husband to church plant, and value my husband's ministry to the church and our family, I am more likely to offer him my help and support. But when I fail to acknowledge the responsibility God has given my husband or put undue pressure on him, thinking of only how it affects me, I am more likely to hinder his work.

My husband has many people who care about him, respect him, and help him lead the church. But he only has one helpmate. I am the only one who listens to his deep discouragement, who satisfies his physical needs, who mothers his children, who is a constant and true companion, who protects his periods of rest, and who values his fruitfulness as much as he does.

> My calling isn't to my husband. It is to God.

Church planting is a "together" calling.

In difficult seasons, I have sought ways to excuse myself from this together calling. I try to convince myself that this is Kyle's calling, his ministry, and that I can do as I like. Or I allow my feathers to be ruffled and fight for my rights, my reputation, and my own (separate) respect. Either way, I grow frustrated when his job requires too much from me.

My calling isn't to my husband. It is to God; church planting is what He's given to me, too. My role looks so much different than my husband's, but it is just as real and just as vital to our together calling.

Staying in the Race

A few years ago, Kyle trained for and ran in the Marine Corps Marathon in Washington, D. C. We decided together that it would be difficult for me to go to D. C. and follow the race with our three small children, so he went alone. However, Kyle received a computer chip for his shoes that would enable me to track his progress online. He also planned to run with his cell phone so family and friends could call and encourage him along the route.

On the morning of the race, I watched his representative red dot steadily trek around a map of D. C. on the marathon's website. At mile 22, however, the red dot stopped moving. I refreshed the web page many times over a twenty-minute stretch and, still, the dot remained frozen on the screen. When I called, frantic, he answered with a weak hello between puffs of breath. He had hit a brick wall, he said, and couldn't run anymore. Hiding my concern, I urged him to keep going, reminding him of the training he had done and how close he was to the finish line. We said goodbye, and I sat transfixed to the computer screen, waiting for the red dot to move again. To my great relief, after a long pause, it moved, inching toward the finish line. Although he had done all the work, I felt some satisfaction knowing that my encouragement had helped him complete the race.

Church planting is like a spiritual and emotional marathon for both the church planter and his wife. Intended as a team race, both must work in tandem to accomplish the God-given goal. The church planter sets the pace and the route for the race as he follows Christ. Ideally, he monitors his racing partner, watching for when she needs refreshment, rest, or encouragement, or if the pace is too grueling and needs adjusting. The church planting wife responds to his leading, matches his stride, and gently informs him of what she needs along the route. As his teammate, the wife encourages, affirms, and helps so that, together, they succeed.

> As church planting wives, we can choose to be either a helper or a hinderer.

Sometimes, though, the church planter and his wife run the marathon with inefficiency and discord. When the church planter sprints ahead of his partner or fails to lead the team, or when the wife argues over the route, criticizes the pace, refuses to run, or goes her own way, they do not run harmoniously and come perilously close to forfeiting the race altogether.

As church planting wives, we cannot control our running partner or the terrain of the race, but we can choose how we respond to our husbands. We can choose to be either a helper or a hinderer. Being a helper or a hinderer is not necessarily about specific acts of service in the home or the church, although these are certainly important. A helper is defined by her heart and attitude with which she responds to her husband and assists him in his calling. We can refuse to open our home to others, speak to him with criticism or disrespect, complain, whine, or demand our way. Or we can respond willingly to his requests, gently and privately address needs or slights, purposefully encourage him, embrace church planting, and exhibit flexibility and joy.

One of the most detrimental ways we hinder our husbands is when we confuse his role with ours. As the leader, he is responsible for the spiritual and emotional health of your family and church. As the helper, we come alongside, helping him flesh out the vision. So often we, the helpmates, look for our husbands to help *us*. We clamor for his attention, for our needs to be met, or to do our own thing, unhindered by church planting's demands. We complain about having to do even the smallest of things to help him. We bristle at being stuck with the behind-the-scenes helper role rather than the limelight leader role. We protect our interests rather than sacrificially giving to our husbands. These are the heart attitudes of a hinderer: fighting (often against the church or the calling) for rights, complaining, criticizing, and refusing to support her husband.

We also hinder our husbands when we wait for him to meet our needs before we meet his. Our role is not dependent on what our husbands do or don't do. We must cultivate a helping heart, seeking to meet his needs, because it is what *God* asks of us. In the end, we help our husbands as a means of serving the Lord.

How *Can* We Help?

As church planting wives, how can we best help our husbands?

Before my husband was a church planter, he was on staff at an established church where his role and responsibilities were firm and clear, which made it relatively easy to prioritize our marriage and family before ministry. His clearly defined role also took the guesswork out of determining how I could help him. He was a college pastor so I taught a college girls' Bible study and discipled college students. His structured schedule provided an unchanging framework for our family and for my week.

Then we planted a church.

Suddenly, ministry threatened to encroach on every aspect of our lives. My husband carried the heavy burden of starting and growing a church, and I felt uncertain about how I could best help him. His job description became "Everything" and mine became "Helpmate to the Man Who Does Everything."

What *does* it mean to be a helpmate to a man who is a church planter?

First, let's define it by what it does *not* mean.

Being the helpmate to a church planter
does not mean that we are helpmates to the church.

We are not married to the church. We are not pastors. We are not on staff. We are not on call for the people of the church. We are not the catchall person for ministries or tasks that need a leader. We are not the ones who meet every need or fulfill every responsibility. Our attention goes first to our relationship with God and then to our husbands, children, homes, and then to ministry and work outside the home.

The lines are often fuzzy, but if we become a helpmate to the entire church, we will not be available to our husbands and children, the people who need us most. Someone else can head the children's ministry or do graphic design for the website, but we are the only ones who can be a helpmate to our husbands and a mother to our kids.

Being the helpmate to a church planter does not mean that we are as
equally responsible for the church's success or well-being as our husbands.

A good helpmate passionately cares about what her husband cares about, but does not have an unhealthy concern for it. Although we care deeply about the church and are intimately involved in it, we must recognize the danger in caring too much. If we are overly concerned about the goings-on in the church plant, if our emotions rise and fall according to the state of the church, then we only add to our husband's anxiety level. Our burden should be for the spiritual, physical, and emotional health of our husband as he carries the burden for the spiritual, physical, and emotional health of the church.

My husband and I joke that, as his helpmate, I am the Pastor to the Pastor, but there is actually some accuracy to that description. I can meet his needs for encouragement, prayer, support, and intimacy in ways that others can't. And by doing so, I am vital to his success as a disciple, husband, father, and pastor. There is joy and freedom that come in embracing my role as his helpmate. Without my constant partnership and joyful assistance, his ministry cannot and will not persist.

I've learned what *not* to do through experiences, mistakes, and trial and error. Similarly, I've learned what is most helpful to my husband in his unique calling. At the core are a heart and attitude of joy, respect, and support.

*A church planting wife helps her husband
when she cultivates her relationship with God.*

Cultivating a relationship with God is important for many reasons, some of which we've discovered in previous chapters. As helpmates, relying on the Spirit for our daily sustenance prevents us from developing an unhealthy neediness for our husbands.

In the first year of church planting, I felt extremely needy. Although we had been in ministry for years, church planting was unchartered territory. In addition, I don't usually handle change well so church planting put me on an emotional roller coaster, desperate for encouragement and help. I felt uncertain about my role, about relationships, and wondered if we were going to survive at all. My husband, distracted by stress and uncertainty himself, had little emotional support to offer me. He retreated more and more inside of himself and was less and less available to me. This proved a combustible combination, leading to many difficult conversations and conflicts.

> I felt uncertain about my role, about relationships, and wondered if we were going to survive at all.

One day I realized that, in my uncertainty regarding our circumstances, I was looking to my husband to meet needs that he couldn't humanly meet and was therefore adding undue pressure on him and additional weight onto his burden. When I confessed this tendency to God and to Kyle, and as I turned more consistently to the Lord with my emotional concerns, the pressure on our marriage eased. In addition, I recognized a decreased interest in myself and an increased interest in helping my husband.

Certainly we have some needs that our husbands can meet, such as encouragement, time, and attention. We should not stop communicating with them and asking for what we need. We must, however, take time to prayerfully consider how we're feeling and what our needs are before communicating them. So often I run, overflowing with emotion, to my husband before I stop to consider what my need is or what the Lord might have to say to me about it. I've discovered that if I ask the Lord about it first, He often extends His wisdom and peace into my heart without involving Kyle. He also helps me pinpoint what I need from my husband and how to lovingly communicate those needs to him. God has taught me that I can *ask* Kyle for what I need, but I cannot *expect* him to make everything in my life right or soothe every emotion. God is the only One who has that ability. As I cultivate my relationship with Him, I find my hope and comfort in Christ and am able to joyfully free my husband to carry out his calling.

A church planting wife helps her husband
when she gives him specific encouragement.

When Kyle and I do premarital counseling with young couples, we convey the need to use specific encouragement. To illustrate, we ask the bride and the groom to give each other a compliment. Inevitably, they offer weak pronouncements of love: *You're pretty,* or *I think you're nice,* or *I like your cooking.* We ask them to be more precise and specific, something like: *When you wore that red dress yesterday, you looked stunningly beautiful. I can't stop thinking about you in it.* Or: *When I visited you at work last week, I observed how people responded to you. I am amazed at how good you are at what you do and proud of the respect you've earned through your hard work.* During the first round of compliments, they politely smile and say thank you. The second attempt elicits tears, affection, and other indications of feeling deeply loved.

Celebrate wins, both big and small.

As the helpmate to the church planter, we have countless opportunities to embolden our husbands through specific encouragement, whether it's about his leadership in the home or his service to the church. Church planting can be discouraging, even for the strongest of leaders. They often second-guess themselves or feel lesser-than. We must resolve to be our husband's biggest cheerleader by showering them with consistent verbal affirmation:

I appreciate how hard you are working to provide for our family.
We have everything we need.
Your sermon today really spoke to me and here's how . . .
You have a tough job, but you do it well.
The way you handled that situation really amazed me.
What you said was perfect and God used it to defuse the conflict.
I am proud to be your wife and thankful for our life together.

Help him see how the Lord is working in your church and through his leadership. Affirm his preaching. Celebrate wins, both big and small. With your encouragement, he will flourish in his leadership of your home and of the church plant.

A church planting wife helps her husband
when she protects his need for rest and retreat.

A few weeks ago, Kyle seemed completely worn out. He had spent several months doing intensive counseling with a couple in our church while fulfilling all of his normal work responsibilities. He was emotionally exhausted, but it was only when I voiced my concern and entreated him to take a break that he acknowledged his need for rest. We decided that he would go away for a portion of a weekend for physical and spiritual rest. It was difficult for me to let him go because I want every last second of him that I can get when he's away from ministry responsibilities, but I knew how good it would be for him. I loved him by sending him away without any complaints. He came back rested, having received the

> Affirm the importance of rejuvenating his spirit and help remove any obstacles that keep him from resting.

refuel he needed from the Lord to press on. He also came back eager to reengage in our marriage and family.

There is only so much encouragement that you can give your husband. Sometimes, like you, his need for encouragement can only be found in the Lord. Recognizing this, a helping heart eagerly carves that time out for him. When you notice his energy and motivation flagging, encourage him to take a personal retreat, rest, or do something that reenergizes him. Affirm the importance of rejuvenating his spirit and help remove any obstacles that keep him from resting, including any guilt he might feel about leaving you and your kids for a few hours or days.

Sometimes helping your husband find time for rest and rejuvenation may mean that you have *less* of it for a time. But you will find that your sacrifice keeps your husband and your marriage healthy and humming.

A church planting wife helps her husband
when she monitors her own schedule.

As we have already seen, the responsibility for the growth and health of the church is not on us. It is not even on our husbands. In 1 Corinthians 3, Paul says that it is the Lord who cultivates growth from the seeds that are planted. In light of this truth, we must not let ourselves become overly burdened or concerned by our husband's work. Doing so leaves us little time and energy for our primary priorities: being a disciple, wife, and mom. We should not be so involved in the ministry that we're always doing "church work" and rising and falling emotionally based upon how the church is doing. A wise helper does not fill her schedule with so many church, community, or social activities that she is too exhausted to give her husband and children what they need. She is selective in what she involves herself in.

At the beginning of the plant, you'll probably do things that you aren't passionate about and that drain you quickly. As soon as you can, hand those things off to a capable leader. It will be better for the church, for you, and for your husband.

I am both a "doer" and an introvert, which is a tricky combination. I stay busy, but I also need time alone to refuel. In particularly busy seasons, alarm bells will go off when I start adding too much to my schedule. When I tell myself that I can handle it or say yes to things just because I feel guilty in saying no, I end up an exhausted, grumpy person who is just trying to survive my schedule. Resentment builds at being pulled in a million directions, so I clamor for rest and have nothing to give my husband and my children. However, when I actually listen to and obey the Spirit's prompting, I find that He often wants me to do less, not more. He helps me say no to unnecessary activities and yes to rest at regular intervals. Then, I am emotionally and physically available to the Lord and to my family. Rather than exhausting myself in a sprint, I can pace myself for the marathon of church planting.

A church planting wife helps her husband
when she is wise in conversation.

Sometimes, in the middle of a conversation about ministry, I notice my husband becoming distracted and withdrawn. I have learned this often means that he doesn't want to talk about church anymore. A helper is wise in conversation, careful about how much she talks about church matters with her husband and purposeful to engage him in conversation that has nothing to do with his work. She refrains from pressing for details as a protection for her marriage and her own heart. She knows that constantly talking about the church plant creates an unhealthy sense of responsibility for her and provides opportunities to critique or criticize her husband.

It is important for us to monitor how much we share with our husbands about our own struggles with church planting.

As church planting wives, it is unnecessary for us to know every detail about every decision. It *is* important for us to encourage our husbands and respect them by trusting them with decisions. A wise husband will often ask for his wife's input, but a wise wife *waits for him to ask* for her evaluation of a situation or feedback on a sermon. I have learned the hard way that when I give my opinion without him first asking for it, he feels attacked and unsupported. As his helpmate, I can and should help him see his blind spots, but my approach needs to be loving and gentle; otherwise he won't hear anything but criticism.

Finally, in regard to being a wise helpmate in conversation, it is important for us to monitor how much we share with our husbands about our own struggles with church planting. If we are constantly complaining, they may take it personally or feel guilty about what God has called them to do. Again, a wise helpmate will take her concerns and struggles to the Lord first and ask for discernment for what needs to be shared.

A church planting wife helps her husband
when she values intimacy.

Before we committed to church planting, Kyle and I attended a helpful church planting conference. During the wives' breakout session, the speaker said, "As you start planting the church, expect to have a lot of sex." We all laughed, but then she explained: "Your husband will not feel successful at much of anything in those first few months. You can encourage him and help him feel successful by responding to his physical touch." I stored that tidbit away, intent on meeting my husband's needs.

She was right.

Intimacy is a powerful reminder to your husband that you value, love, and need him. In church planting, there aren't many other avenues for him to receive those things, so you are a wise helpmate when you respond to him physically.

A church planting wife helps her husband
when she prays for him.

Finally, but perhaps most importantly, we must pray for our husbands. They have taken on a daunting task. Because they are fighting spiritual battles, they need supernatural protection, discernment, wisdom, and leadership in order to accomplish everything they do each day. The only way we can help in that spiritual battle is by praying for them.

Sometimes we erroneously believe that being a helpmate makes us small or less useful in the kingdom, but in God's economy the servant is elevated to the primary position. With Jesus as our example, the role of servant is one of honor and esteem. We are most like Him when we are helping our husbands by serving and sacrificing for them.

As a church planting wife with a helping heart, there is return for your work. When you help your husband, he has more to give you. When you embrace his spiritual and emotional leadership in the home and the church, he will be more likely to lovingly lead and protect you.

While we desire to have our needs met by our husbands, the return we receive from God is of much more importance. After all, the help we offer our husbands is ultimately an offering to Him. If we desire to please Him, we will sacrifice for Him. A natural outflow of a dependent and sacrificial heart toward God will be a helping heart toward our husbands. As faithful helpers—the role He's called us to—we will experience joy and God's pleasure.

So now the question again: What is your heart toward your husband? Are you a hinderer or a helper?

Cultivating Your Heart

This chapter discusses many practical ways in which you can help your husband. Your role is unique—others will take helping and/or leadership positions in the church, but as your husband's wife, you have a position no one else has.

Review the areas of helping mentioned in this chapter and evaluate which are strengths and which need improvement.

Prioritizing your husband and children before the church
Letting him take the responsibility for the success of the plant
Encouraging him in specific ways
Protecting his need for rest and retreat
Monitoring your own schedule
Using wisdom in conversation
Valuing intimacy with your husband
Praying for him

Would you say that, overall, you're a helper or a hinderer? Is there an action or a change you can make today?

Interview with

Shauna
Pilgreen

*Shauna is married to Ben Pilgreen, church planting pastor of
Epic Church, a thriving church in the heart of San Francisco.
Shauna is also a mother to three boys, an author, and a contributor
to Flourish.me, an online ministry to pastors' wives.*

What advice would you give to ministers' wives who are just starting out?

First of all, this is one vocation that works best when you, the wife, are fully supportive and engaged in your husband's ministry. You don't have to be actively involved in everything "church," nor are you in ministry to please the entire congregation. However, you did marry this man! So, since you said *I do,* supporting your husband's dream and vision in ministry falls under your marriage covenant.

Second, communicate with your husband. He needs your attention, support, and verbal commitment. Give him room to share his fears, dreams, and vision. But you need his attention, too! Ask him to be open to hear your fears, dreams, and vision about ministry. Discuss how your dreams can come alongside his dreams and how the two of you will serve each other before you serve the church.

Give an example of how you've tried to support your husband in ministry.

In November 2008, Ben shared his dream with me of starting a church in a strategic urban setting. (I believe I was trying to relax in the bathtub at the time!) He was then serving as a teaching pastor at a strong missional church in the Midwest. I told him I would spend the next few days praying about this with him and for us. Ten days later, I said, "I'm in!" I meant: *I'm on board. I agree to this with you. With a clear mind and a focused heart, this is what I think the Lord is calling us to do.* I didn't mean: *Everything must be laid out in front of us before I take the next step. Or I'll do this on certain conditions.*

We talked long about how this would affect our three boys (then five, three, and one), our extended family, our current church family/staff, and our marriage. We made a list of nonnegotiables, things we would NOT sacrifice. On that list: our marriage, date nights, a happy and joy-filled childhood for our boys, our personal faith journeys with God. What were we willing to sacrifice? Owning a home, having two cars, living near extended family.

What has been the hardest part about being a minister's wife for you and how have you handled that?

Sharing Ben. I relate being a pastor's wife to being a doctor's wife. Our husbands are on call 24/7. I share Ben with every person who walks through the doors of our church. I share him with our church staff (people I adore). I share him with our partnering churches.

I'd like to say that though this was/is the hardest part for me, I have handled it like a good wife. That I have blown him kisses each time he has had to hurry out the door. That I welcome the sound of a text message at dinnertime. In my flesh, I am outraged at the demands of ministry at times. There have even been times when sharing Ben has caused me to cocoon with my boys in our home and shut out the world. Then I step back and remember that it's not about me. I recall our initial talks of ministry. I remind myself to whom I belong and that my self-worth is not tied to the gives-and-takes of this vocation. I grab hold of the truth that Ben loves me and has not sacrificed a "nonnegotiable" by running out the door or responding to a text. He is simply loving others and meeting needs.

I have to confess my selfishness. I have to rebuild and re-declare my support, love, and partnership with Ben. This does leave a mark, like all sin can. If I'm not careful, it not only leaves a mark on my husband's heart but also the hearts of our community. Because Ben loves me so much, he'd sacrifice his ministry for his family. If he were to think that I was unhappy in this ministry life, he'd leave it in a heartbeat.

Truth be told, I get the most of Ben. He's home for dinner. He wrestles with the boys when he gets home so I can put the meal on the table. He takes me out on dates. He greets me and the boys when we arrive at church. He calls and texts me throughout the day. He has my best interests at heart.

CHAPTER FOUR

the Connected Heart

DEVELOPING LIFE-GIVING FRIENDSHIPS

When it comes to friendship, I have developed a great deal of insecurity.

In high school and college, I enjoyed close relationships with other women in which we shared the intimate details of our lives. Something strange occurred, however, when I graduated into adulthood, got married, and entered the ministry with my husband.

Relationships Change

Although most of my high school and college friends lived in different cities and states, our relationships continued. But in our new city and new church, I struggled to make new friends. At first, in the bright-eyed honeymoon stage of marriage, I didn't prioritize friendship, so this new dearth of relationships didn't bother me much. After a few years, though, I noticed a subtle loneliness creeping into my heart. Because I had not cultivated friendships, I felt almost emotionally malnourished. Worse, insecurity began plaguing my interactions with other women, leaving me self-conscious and concerned that my lack of friendships must indicate that I'm somehow not likeable. I felt as if I'd forgotten how to be a friend, how to make friends, or how to share myself with others. As a result, in our first eight years of marriage and ministry, I cried more tears of loneliness than any other kind.

To Know and Be *Known*

I don't think this struggle is unusual for women in ministry, but I also don't think it unusual for *all* women. I've spoken with women of all life stages and situations who have bemoaned their lack of heart friends. Every woman desires connection with others in which they are known, accepted, understood, and loved.

However, I do believe that ministry life exacerbates the struggle. One reason is that somewhere, somehow an idea developed that ministry wives should not have friends in the church. Jen Hatmaker, a church planting wife in Austin, shared with me about this idea:

> At my wedding shower when I was nineteen years old, my pastor's wife who I loved and respected gave a talk, and she looked me in the eyes and said, "When we were in seminary, John's professors told him not to make close friends because it would create jealousy in the church and people would resent us. They said part of our sacrifice was to be each other's best friend to the exclusion of outside couples and families, in order to preserve harmony in our congregation.
>
> "I want to tell you something," she continued. "Do the exact opposite of that. Have best friends. Take trips together. Be vulnerable with them. Let love in and give it out with abandon. Have friends closer than brothers and sisters. I've been lonely my entire life, and I want your future life in ministry to be so full of close friends and love, you can barely contain it."
>
> I did exactly that. I spend so much time with my friends, it's embarrassing. It's this simple: I don't put any "should" or "should nots" into this equation because my husband is a pastor. I'm a girl. I love my friends just like every girl does.

Added Demands

Beyond lifestyle-induced isolation, other people's assumptions sometimes create problems for the church planting wife. If the reason for church planting is unclear, or if the church planter and his wife are put on a pedestal reserved for superspiritual Christians, the church planting wife might feel misunderstood or deemed unapproachable. As a result, other women may not let down their guard or share who they really are, creating a barrier to intimate friendship.

In addition, church planting wives confront friendship struggles resulting from relocation, distance from familiar support systems, cultural differences, greater ministry time demands, being an outsider, or an inability to talk about their discouragement with people involved in the church plant. It comes as no surprise, then, that church planting wives report that making friends is one of the greatest struggles and heartaches they have:

- 65% of church planting wives say their husbands provide their primary emotional support
- 59% of church planting wives are busy leading one to three major ministries in the church in addition to family, community, and personal commitments and have little time for friendship cultivation
- 56% of pastors' wives report having no close friends
- 80% report having struggled with depression[6]

Ministry: The Ultimate Excuse?

We can list all the reasons why church planting makes friendship difficult, but most of the time, if we're honest, we use ministry as an excuse. We blame church planting for our loneliness while we habitually withhold our needs from others or refuse to let people serve us. We think and talk about how we do not lead a "normal" life, fueling our own assumptions that we are different than everyone else, that no one understands our lives, and that we are all alone. Victimlike, we resign ourselves to an unwelcome fate of friendlessness and isolation.

I can't be friends with people in the church since I can't talk to them about one of the biggest aspects of my life.

No one understands what my life is like as a church planter's wife.

No one initiates conversation with me, therefore they must not like me.

People will eventually leave the church so I can't get connected to anyone or I'll just be hurt in the end.

We're eventually going to leave so I don't want to get too connected.

People expect me to be a certain way, so since I can't be myself, I'm just going to retreat away from them.

> I tried sharing my heart and her response wasn't what I hoped it would be. I don't think I'll try that again.

I'm tired of always being the initiator/shower planner/leader/hostess. No one ever does anything for me.

I can't share or show my faults and weaknesses because I'm the pastor's wife.

I should always be giving or leading; I'm not entitled to receive.

I tried sharing my heart and her response wasn't what I hoped it would be. I don't think I'll try that again.

If I share my needs, I will be a burden to others.

When we make these assumptions or believe these lies, we can slip into self-pity, creating our own isolation. They become excuses for retreat or self-induced isolation. Blaming ministry only serves to erect further barriers to friendship.

That's exactly what I did for too many years. My circumstances—serving in a somewhat age-isolated ministry and having three babies right in a row—made friendship difficult, but I made it even more challenging by letting my circumstances (and my insecurities) dictate my life. Looking back, I can clearly pinpoint how I could have done things differently. And, thankfully, through church planting, God gave me a do-over.

Stay in the Water

After we visited Charlottesville for the first time, we returned home with the assurance that God was calling us to this city and with an eagerness to share our vision with others in hopes that they might join us. We welcomed friends and ministry partners into our home for coffee and dessert, showed them pictures of the city, and shared about its spiritual needs. Before Kyle communicated his vision for the church we hoped to start, he invited the group to dream for a moment about the kind of church they'd like to be a part of. The group shared things that resonated with me: authentic community, a gospel focus, and a missions orientation. I wanted all those things too, but more than anything, I wanted to be in a church where I was known, where I was not just the "pastor's wife" but simply another person included in the inner workings of the church body. I knew this was my opportunity for a friendship do-over, so when Kyle asked that question of the group, I mostly thought about my desire for community with others. I no longer wanted to be on the outside looking in. I wanted to be in the thick of messy, dynamic, give-and-take relationships; knowing and being known in a safe, grace-filled community of faith. I prayed that my friendless season of life would give way to a season full of life-giving relationships.

Being physically distant from family and friends didn't help. Being in a new city was fun, but draining.

Though church planting can be isolating and relationship-poor, it has its advantages. One of the biggest is that, as church planter and wife, we have great influence on the environment of the church. We can help create an atmosphere of warmth, unity, community, and openness, where all life stages interact together. We have a part in implanting deep, Christlike friendships into the nature of the church and, in a sense, creating an environment for our own friendships to grow.

When we started our church plant, I resolved to pursue friendships differently and, at first, my pursuit yielded little fruit. To my great discouragement, for the first year of the plant, our church filled out with newly married couples, young singles, and college students. I thoroughly enjoyed my relationships with these people, but I knew, being ten years younger, they saw me more as a mentor than as a friend. As they built community through late-night movie excursions or meals out, I stayed home with my husband and children.

Being physically distant from family and friends didn't help. Being in a new city was fun, but draining. Starting over relationally left me once again feeling needy, unsure of myself, and exhausted.

I expressed my frustration to God about this. Was He really going to allow a replay of the utter loneliness I'd felt in our previous church? My ideal picture of glorious unity and community in church planting was dying a quick death.

I wish I could say that God beamed down the perfect friend, the ideal small group, or an issue-free community of faith. He didn't. He did, however, grace our church with families one year into the church plant. After time and effort, these women have become friends. I also wish I could say that I have got this friend thing figured out, that I never feel lonely or isolated anymore. But I don't have it all figured out. Friendship continues to be something I pray about, seek, and sometimes stress about even as I look around and see the warm relationships growing around me.

In a sense, this has become my friendship philosophy: continue on, keep trying, initiate, remain open, persevere. If I cast aside my insecurities and refuse to give up, in due time, friendship will happen. And it has. But I've learned that it will never be easy. Friendship will always require my effort.

I imagine it like a river with a steady current. Regarding friendship, I am wading into the river, bombarded by a current of circumstances and insecurities, sometimes even frustrations. I can choose to give up my attempts at relationships with others and float along until I'm deposited into a stagnant pool of depression, isolation, disconnection, or loneliness. Or I can continue to work against the current by initiating, responding, appreciating, praying, sharing, asking, letting in, inviting, encouraging, receiving, and so many other actions that move us farther upstream to where we want to be—connected.

If we wait around for it to just *happen*, it probably won't. If we expect friendships to be perfect, we will be disappointed. If we search for that one friend who will meet all our friendship needs, we will never have any. So it is important, if we desire friendship, that we work at it, moving against the current toward connection.

In my fight upstream, I have learned lessons about friendship that have carried me against the current. I hope they encourage your own pursuit.

Friendship Is a Gift of Grace

Aside from the logistical issues of marriage, children, and work responsibilities that make connecting difficult, why are adult friendships so hard?

Thinking on this question, I was reminded of Dietrich Bonhoeffer's thoughts on Christian community in *Life Together*:

> It is easily forgotten that the fellowship of Christian brethren is a gift of grace, a gift of the Kingdom of God that any day may be taken from us, that the time that still separates us from utter loneliness may be brief indeed. Therefore, let him who until now has had the privilege of living a common Christian life with other Christians praise God on his knees and declare: It is grace, nothing but grace, that we are allowed to live in community with Christian brethren.[7]

In other words, we are not guaranteed or entitled to heart friends. They are gifts of grace, and when we catch glimpses of sisterly love, we must receive it as such with deep gratitude.

Bonhoeffer doesn't say it, but his words imply it: friendship does not come easily. We tend to believe the myth that friendship should be easy, requires little effort, or, most debilitating, that we're the only one who is having such a hard time with friendship.

Friendship is a gift that God loves to give.

Why doesn't God make it easier on us? After all, He calls us to live in community with others, to let our love for one another be a light to those in darkness. I prayed to Him for *years* for a good friend where I lived, but didn't see His answer. I believe He allowed those seasons of friendship dryness so that I would not put anyone else in His place, so that I would rely on Him to meet my deepest needs. Through that season, I also developed an eye and a compassion for the women standing on the fringe longing for connection.

Friendship is a gift that God loves to give. In fact, the primary way He grows, challenges, and encourages us is through other believers. As we cultivate friendship with God, He shows us who needs our friendship and gives us discernment about who we should pursue. In Him, we have a Person who takes our insecurities from us and shows us how to love. He teaches us humility and how to approach relationships with openness and vulnerability, a necessary ingredient for friendship.

When we understand that friendship is a gift of grace, our hearts refrain from growing resentful and bitter when the connections don't seem to be there. We can wait expectantly for it, looking for where it may come. We also acknowledge and appreciate the small acts of friendship that come our way: a phone call, a note, or an invitation.

There is no ideal friend or church community. We can't place unrealistic expectations on ourselves or on others, thinking that they will satisfy all our deepest longings for connections. Relationships— even Christian friendships—are messy, challenging, and imperfect. They are gifts of grace and we should receive them as such, not demand from them more than they are able to give us.

Where to Start?

While God gives the gift of friendship, we also play a role in developing friends. When we use ministry or insecurity as an excuse, we tend to wait for other women to initiate friendship with us. If we desire friendship, however, we cannot wallow in self-pity, wishing friends would fall from the sky or focus on what we lack or what we wish others would do for us. We must resolve to initiate consistently and do so with a genuine interest in others. When we focus more on meeting the needs of others and blessing them rather than our wants and needs, we sow seeds of friendship. This idea is really just a scriptural principle applied to friendship:

And let us consider one another in order to stir up love and good works. (Hebrews 10:24)

Let nothing be done through selfish ambition or conceit, but in lowliness of mind let each esteem others better than himself. Let each of you look out not only for his own interests, but also for the interests of others. (Philippians 2:3–4)

Love . . . does not seek its own. (1 Corinthians 13:5)

God instructs us to actively put others before ourselves. He models this love, as He gives to us without expectation of love being returned. Out of an overflow of God's love, then, we must love those we have a natural affinity for and those we don't, those who admire us and those who don't, those who approve of us and those who may not. In other words, we treat people with honor and respect. As we do so, we invite reciprocal friendship. It may not always be returned how we would like, but those seeds of friendship sow a bounty in our hearts:

> Inviting others into our homes is the first step toward inviting them into our hearts.

But this I say: He who sows sparingly will also reap sparingly, and *he who sows bountifully will also reap bountifully*. (2 Corinthians 9:6)

One man gives freely, yet gains even more; another withholds unduly, but comes to poverty. A generous man will prosper, *he who refreshes others will himself be refreshed*. (Proverbs 11:24–25 NIV)

Give, and it will be given to you. A good measure, pressed down, shaken together and running over, will be poured into your lap. For with the measure you use, it will be measured to you. (Luke 6:38 NIV)

This is certainly not a formula where, like a vending machine, we put in some effort and a friend pops out. The point is that our generosity will bring us joy, keep us from isolation and self-pity, and, as we show interest in others, help us build connections and extend invitations for friendship.

Hospitality is a great avenue for establishing relational connections because inviting others into our homes is the first step toward inviting them into our hearts. Unfortunately, instead of using hospitality as an extension of friendship, we tend to put too much pressure on ourselves to create the perfect home or meal for guests. Meant to create relationships, hospitality instead becomes something we fear and avoid because of our insecurities.

I know those insecurities.

I make it a rule never to read lifestyle magazines because even glancing at the covers in the checkout line at the grocery store makes my blood pressure go up. *Should I be making my own butter?* I ask myself as I put the Doritos on the conveyor belt. I am especially stressed out by the recipes, party suggestions, and table decorations. It's all way too perfect. And that says something coming from a recovering perfectionist.

But is this the goal in hospitality? To have place cards, expensive centerpieces, handmade party favors, and beautiful table linens? Should we only invite people into our homes when we finally get our lives perfectly together?

Our culture's version of hospitality involves beautiful events with beautiful decor for beautiful people. It's too bad that we often believe this is true hospitality and therefore don't invite others into our homes. When we don't practice hospitality regularly, we miss opportunities to hear people's stories, to be known, and to display and experience a tangible gospel. We miss opportunities for friendship.

We miss these opportunities because we worry about the size of our space, the decor in our home, the cleanliness of the bathrooms, or our ability to cook. Hospitality is not about setting a scene or a table. It's about connecting over a meal and opening ourselves to relationships. It says: Here is my carpet covered in Cheerios, several invariably smashed. Here are the dirty dishes in the sink. Here is a pretty basic meal (or takeout). Here are my rambunctious children. And here I am. You are welcome in my home and in my heart. Paul could have been speaking to church planting wives in need of friendship when he said, "Be kindly affectionate to one another with brotherly love . . . distributing to the needs of the saints, given to hospitality" (Romans 12:10, 13).

Open and Vulnerable

To reiterate, inviting people into our homes is a bridge builder for friendship and the gospel. However, if we invite them into our homes without allowing them into our hearts, we miss the point of hospitality. In order to build friendships, we must also allow our weaknesses and struggles to show. We must be warm, vulnerable, and accessible, not closed-off emotionally.

Sometimes this takes practice, especially for those of us used to leading, serving, and meeting the needs of others.

As a recovering perfectionist, I sometimes confuse holiness and perfection. Rather than try to reflect on God's grace or allow its natural compelling work in my life (holiness), I try really hard to do godly things, produce spiritual fruit, and live a neatly tied-up life (perfection).

I practice letting people see my house in various states of disarray.

Sometimes I do this because I believe God can't love me without my efforts, but most of the time I do this because I am trying to fulfill some arbitrary Christian standard that I think others expect of me or that I expect of myself. I feel like a walk-in freezer forever attempting to keep myself at a constant, controlled temperature.

I grow weary of myself, of maintaining my frozen image.

Sometimes, to thaw out, I practice letting people see me in various states of disarray. When a friend is dropping off her children to play, I purposely do not change out of my bright-red, extra-large moose pajama pants and do not fix my hair or makeup.

I practice asking for help, even when I can likely do it on my own and even though I must ignore the feelings of guilt over being such a burden to everyone.

I practice telling my friends the sorry state of my heart—how I envy, how I don't trust God sometimes, how I am restless, and how I grow discontent.

I practice letting people see my house in various states of disarray, because that somehow feels even more intimate than showing them my heart or letting them see me in those awful pajamas.

I practice not cleaning the ring from the toilet bowl and not fussing over an elaborate meal when friends are coming over. And then I practice leaving the garage door up so they will walk through the jumble of bikes and coats and backpacks and leaves blown in rather than climbing the stairs to my beautifully arranged porch.

I practice not hiding from other moms the Cheetos and the juice boxes I allow my children to ingest.

I practice letting my children draw all over the windows with window markers (and then I practice not immediately digging under the sink for the Windex when they run upstairs to play).

I am not always prepared for people to see me or my home in differing stages of disorder, but I am secretly glad when they do. Like when one of the other pastors at our church showed up one morning last week at the kitchen door as I was doing dishes in my red moose pajama pants and previous day's makeup. I was a smeared, moosey mess and so was the kitchen, but instead of running to hide in my room, I said hello and returned to the dishes with a smile. *Good,* I thought to myself. *I'm getting better. I'm thawing.*

I'm practicing thawing, too—not worrying when others see my disarray on accident, even when I am not controlling what messes they're allowed to see.

In thawing, I find myself in a state of gratefulness. Less of my time is spent corralling life and more of it is spent seeing, listening, and relating. There is less coldness and looking inward, more warmth and seeing outward. Less trying to impress and more enjoying the life and people I love.

Sometimes I am not good at gratefulness. Sometimes I don't let God's grace flood my heart because it reminds me that I actually need it, and that I can't do it all. Sometimes I care more about the state of my home than the state of my heart.

But I'm practicing, and my friendships are better for it.

Finding Friends

It may sound strange, but I have a hard time pinpointing who my friends are.

Each week, I spend time with various kinds of people in different situations, both official ministry events and informal social situations.

Many of these people attend our church, and often we talk together about intimate things. But sometimes the lines between ministry and friendship become blurred. Am I having coffee with a friend or am I having coffee with someone who needs counsel? Is this a person who desires to know me or who desires to know the "pastor's wife"?

Most of the time I can distinguish between the two easily, but sometimes I can't. I've discovered, however, that when *I* have physical, emotional, or spiritual needs, the lines become clearly drawn. Who can I count on to listen, to pray for me, to carry some of the burden with me, even ministry burdens? *Who can I trust?*

My friend Jessica unknowingly helped me develop a friendship litmus test a few weeks ago when she had her third child. With three children under three, she confessed her difficulty in getting out of the house and asked if I would be willing to run an errand for her. She then handed me a broken nursing bra to exchange at the mall. As I left with her nursing bra, I realized that not only did she trust me with her money, but she also felt completely comfortable handing me her underwear. Women don't ask just anyone to do that. In that moment, holding a broken bra in my hands, I felt privileged and extremely thankful that she would consider me her friend. I also recognized this as my litmus test for friendship. Who, I wondered, would I ask to exchange a nursing bra for me? Or more accurately, since I no longer need nursing bras (sigh), who would I ask to carry a heavy personal burden for me?

A few faces immediately popped in my head. When I interact with these women, I leave feeling refreshed and full of life. They ask about me. They know my needs, my concerns, my faults, my joys. They share their own with me, even their doubts and weaknesses.

Sometimes, though, I have a difficult time pinpointing friendship because I'm looking for that one, catchall friend, like the best friend I had growing up. Thinking my adult friendships will look like my high school or college friendships, I don't always have eyes to see friends right in front of me. I put way too many parameters on friendship: they have to go to my church, they have to have the same-age kids, I have to like their husband, they can't be in a different life stage, they have to be on the same page spiritually.

I don't have one friend who is all of those things to me. I have Jo, my lifelong friend, who doesn't relate to me as a "pastor's wife." I have Melanie, who makes me laugh and whose family connects well with mine. I have Jessica, who prays for me and asks me good questions. I have Marylyn, who encourages me. I have Emily, who shares similar struggles and tastes with me. I have Aimee, a neighbor with similarly aged kids. I have Claire, a mentor and listening ear. I have Lacy, a fellow pastor's wife. I am loved well by these women, and I hope I am a blessing to them, too. But when I look for one person to be my best friend, I fail to see the blessings of these different kinds of friends: fun friends, good conversation friends, encouraging friends, and praying friends.

If you're new to church planting and to your city, you may not be able to pinpoint those friends yet. Consider who God is knitting your heart with. Acknowledge, appreciate, and cultivate the friendships God is trying to give you. Who are trustworthy women that you can open up with? Whose company do you enjoy? Who would you like to get to know better? Who gives you life when you spend time with them? Get past the idea of an ideal, all-encompassing friend, stop using ministry as an excuse, take initiative, and extend invitations into your home and heart.

Investing in Others

Certainly, if you have God's eyes for others, He will also lead you to invest in younger women through discipleship relationships. Over time, these women will become special friends to you as you watch them grow and experience life together.

When our church was still in its infancy, a young woman named Emily visited one Sunday. Not knowing us or anyone attending, she appeared nervous and uncomfortable. When she left, I doubted if she would return. But she did, eventually becoming an essential member of our core team and one of our first community group leaders. Emily and I connected easily, and I sensed that she was ripe for discipleship. I invited her to coffee and asked her to join me in a discipleship relationship. She accepted and, over the course of the next year, we met weekly for breakfast. Clearly, God placed us together because of our commonalities and similar struggles. It was a joy to watch her grow and a blessing to have someone to share my life with during that season of our church plant. By the end of the year, Emily became a friend.

In fact, discipleship has been God's primary tool in helping me grow and develop friendships. Not all of these relationships turn into friendships, but some do, and for those I am extremely thankful.

I have also noticed that as I have encouraged others to invest in discipleship relationships, a sense of connection and Spirit-filled community has filled our church. Because deep relationships are the norm, I have reaped the benefits of other discipleship relationships.

Investing in the Community

We cannot only seek comfortable, easy friendships. We must also pursue relationships with unbelievers and outsiders.

Being in ministry sometimes feels like getting sucked into a church vortex. We rush from church services to small groups to potluck fellowships to prayer meetings to conferences to Bible study each week and then, come Sunday, start the cycle again.

When Kyle and I announced to our previous church that we were leaving to plant a church in another state, our next-door neighbor stopped us one evening when we were outside and told us how excited he was for our new venture. We were a bit confused how he knew about it, seeing as how we didn't really know him and often had trouble remembering his name. So we asked how he knew we were moving. "Oh, I go to your church." Kyle and I accepted his congratulations, walked inside, and looked at each other in disbelief: *He goes to our church? He's lived next door for years and we never even knew his name, much less that he went to our church?*

I remember lying in bed that night, ashamed. Here we were about to church plant and we had not even bothered to get to know our neighbors. We were so engrossed in our Christian circles that we had lost touch with the real world around us. I determined that, church planting or no church planting, I never would let that happen again.

But now that we have lived in Charlottesville for several years and our church is less church plant and more real honest-to-goodness church, I am starting to feel the pull again. Church planting starts with a focus on the outsiders, but when our church grows, it is easy to lose sight of how we can connect with them. How easy it is to enjoy the warmth of hard-earned Christian fellowship and leave the world outside the circle we have created. It is a difficult balance keeping one foot in the local community and one foot in Christian community.

Jesus said, "As you go make disciples . . ." Friendships with those outside the church await us where God already has us, such as in our neighborhood, workplace, through our kids' sports teams, moms groups, PTO, book clubs, and community organizations. These relationships require initiation and invitation and sometimes come at great sacrifice to us, but they are avenues for the gospel to go forward into our communities.

Be Curious

Aside from quieting my insecurities and taking initiative, the most important thing I've learned about friendship is simply to be curious.

For example, every time I'm with my friend Alexis, I pepper her with questions about her life, her thoughts, her experiences. Of all my friends, she is the most unlike me, or unlike any of my other friends for that matter. Alexis is not a Christian, nor does she have any previous church experience. In her world, I am an anomaly, not only because I am a pastor's wife but because I believe in Jesus and because I talk with her about my belief. We have great conversations, Alexis and I, about our families, the effects of divorce, the men in our lives, friendship, and about our goals and passions.

Although we have little in common, we share a mutual respect for each other. We also share, I've discovered, a deep curiosity about other people. Our friendship has developed and is fueled by this shared curiosity, by this willingness to step into the other's shoes, to understand the other's perspective.

When we are together, our conversations have at the core an abiding wonder: What is it like to be you?

After years of ministry, I've discovered that everyone has a story. If I am simply curious about others, if I show genuine interest in them, I *always* find that they, in some way, have walked or are walking a hard, broken road.

Spirit-led curiosity is our greatest ally in life, in ministry, and in friendship. Before I understood the gospel and its extravagant grace, I feared knowing and being known. What if I heard their stories of walking the hard, broken road and didn't have answers? What if the gospel couldn't handle their hurts? What if they heard mine and found me lacking? What if grace might not apply? I simply could not sit in the paradox of simultaneous brokenness and grace.

The gospel allows us the freedom, however, to listen and not have all the answers, to ask questions and not have to preach, to speak honestly and not recite formulaic responses, to hear and not make judgments, *to love freely*. The gospel is life; it brings life.

Curiosity about others is not busybody information gathering but a Philippians 2:1-4 interest, where we seek to understand the context beyond what we see on the surface, where we gently uncover hidden shame, where we actively bless others right where they are, all so that we might bring the light of the gospel into the hard, broken road.

This kind of curiosity about others prevents so many of our own dysfunctions. An others-interest keeps us from thinking too much about ourselves or being indifferent to the plights of those around us. It prevents our misguided comparisons, categorizations, jealousies, and assumptions. It thwarts our discontentment because we become fully aware that no one is exempt from the difficult road, *that no one has it easy*.

And when we lay aside our own fears of being found out, when we breathe grace, when we reveal ourselves, when we stop our self-focus, we suddenly find countless opportunities to share the gospel, to love, to encourage.

We suddenly find that we aren't alone on the broken road.

Cultivating the Heart

Have you experienced that "somewhere, somehow an idea developed that ministry wives should not have friends in the church"? Does this misguided notion nag at you?

How easy is it for you to

be open and vulnerable?

let someone come in when your house is a mess?

initiate relationships?

try again if you've felt rebuffed?

invest in someone who is younger; less mature spiritually;
    not a believer?

What possible relationships can you make with people outside the church? Do you tend to see everyone you meet as a potential church member, or can you form a friendship for its own sake?

Do you feel you always need to be "on"? How can you relax and just enjoy people?

Reread and meditate on these verses from the chapter. Add others that are helpful: Philippians 2:1–4; Hebrews 10:24; 1 Corinthians 13:5; 2 Corinthians 9:6; Proverbs 11:24–25; Luke 6:38.

Interview with

Brandi
Wilson

Brandi Wilson is married to Pete, who is the senior pastor at Cross Point Church in Nashville, Tennessee. Cross Point was planted in the fall of 2002 and is now a multisite church. She is the co-leader of Leading and Loving It, a ministry created to connect, encourage, and equip pastors' wives and other women in ministry. Pete and Brandi have three boys.

Sometimes I feel pressure to know and share about my life with anyone who shows interest. Do you have any sort of litmus test that helps you determine who you can be open and vulnerable with in your church and who you may need to keep gentle but firm boundaries with?

Having relationships in ministry is risky, but the bigger risk is not having friends and sinking into the depths of isolation.

I believe we were created for life in community. What we have to determine is what that community looks like for us. Some of us choose to have friendships with people on our staff and in our church; others choose their relational investment to be outside of their church community and sometimes outside of their state.

This is how I determine who I am willing to take relationship risks with:

- I take friendships very slowly. I never jump two feet in but start in very small ways to slowly begin to build trust.
- I realize that all relationships have boundaries. Boundaries are healthy. What can make a relationships sticky is when you have a boundary someone else doesn't realize. For instance, I've had friendships before in which I placed some very strong boundaries on what I was willing to share. But the friend chose to tell me everything and believed because they put that trust in me, that I must have told them everything too, which I didn't. And that's a tough place to be.
- I think it's healthy to have friendships at different levels: inner, middle, and outer circles. People who you're willing to tell more to than others. People who you enjoy but probably aren't going

to share in depth with. It's not that you don't appreciate what all friendships have to bring to the table, but it's possible to crave community yet also crave privacy.

• I've discovered that even if we have close friends, we will probably go through seasons of isolation. There will be situations we can't discuss, incidents that we can't get our friend's feedback on, and frustrations that should be kept to ourselves.

When you are working through something related to the church or ministry, like a hurt or discouragement, who do you talk to about those things?

One of the greatest gifts I have received throughout my years in ministry is the people God has placed around me. I have a couple of close friends here in Nashville who are very safe places for me to find encouragement and support. I also have Lori, a senior pastor's wife in Las Vegas. Because our husbands share the same position in our churches, she really understands what struggles and discouragements we might be facing. Having a friend outside of our church has been such a gift. She doesn't live here, she doesn't know these people, she's an outside source who can take my frustrations and pain without relating them to someone she knows.

Now that Cross Point Church has grown so much, how do you still pursue relationships with nonbelievers in your community?

Two main places where I am able to interact with nonbelievers are our local YMCA and our children's school. The school my children are zoned for is actually in another county where we (as of yet) don't currently have a campus, so few people know I am the pastor's wife. I'm just Jett, Gage, and Brewer's mom. Also, the sports teams they play on are built around their school community, which means we're getting to spend some weekend time with folks outside our normal sphere of influence.

Do you find that sometimes people are intimidated by you or feel they can't be themselves around you because you're the "pastor's wife"? How do you break those barriers? How do you help people know you and feel at ease around you?

I'm a big believer of just being yourself, of being comfortable in your own skin. My greatest personal struggle in fifteen years of ministry has been just being comfortable being me and not allowing myself to be shaped by the expectations of others or the expectations I had for myself.

I love the way it is said in Galatians 6:4–5 (The Message):
Make a careful exploration of who you are and the work you have
been given, and then sink yourself into that. Don't be impressed with
yourself. Don't compare yourself with others. Each of you must take
responsibility for doing the creative best you can with your own life.

the Sacrificial Heart

ERADICATING PRIDE

In church planting, there is a constant, uncomfortable battle that rages inside of me. It is not the big or dramatic: Will I *go*? Will I follow God's call? Does my life and all it encompasses—my marriage, my children, my ministry, my writing—belong to Him?

The constant battle is more subtle, more everyday, more *hideable*. At the center is one question: *Will I sacrifice?* Or as Oswald Chambers poses in *My Utmost for His Highest*: "[Am I] willing to spend and be spent; not seeking to be ministered unto, but to minister?"[8]

Will I or Won't I?

This sacrifice question wasn't answered one time: upon entry into seminary, upon my husband's acceptance of a ministry position, or upon our church's launch date. The question is answered every day, every time we put our hands to the plow, every time someone comes with a concern, every time something is required of me. It's a question regarding my heart: Will I or won't I? Will I pour out my life as a fragrant offering before the Lord for the benefit of others, or will I seek to have my own needs met, seek what's comfortable, pursue appreciation, and seek attention? Will I look for people to bless me or look for ways to bless others? Will I serve out of obligation and duty or will I serve people like I'm serving God Himself? Am I in this for God to use me or for *me to use God?*

The sacrifice question must be answered every day, because ministry is not so much the big, dramatic acts of sacrifice but the little, unseen ones. So true!

Because we can do all manner of ministry activities and never be a living sacrifice, poured out for the benefit of others.

Because we are so easily deceived to think we can live for ourselves and be faithful to God.

In church planting, I have answered the sacrifice question more than any other. Sometimes I get it right, but sometimes I don't.

One Sunday early in our church planting experience stands out as a time I got it wrong. On that day, I stood at the door, chatting with people as they left the service. My children ran circles around me, occasionally stopping to ask when we could go home. As the school gym where we meet emptied, I noticed that there were few people putting away chairs or equipment. A glance down the hall confirmed that the hospitality tables and children's area also needed to be put away. Reluctantly, I began folding tablecloths, taking tables down, putting away equipment, and throwing trash away. No one offered to help me, even as my children whined and tugged at me. Frustration mounted. My initial annoyance that no one was helping clean up gave way to ugly self-pity.

> Sacrifice? What for? All I could think about was myself. It was not my finest moment.

I have been setting up and tearing down long before these people even knew this church existed. It's someone else's turn.

I shouldn't have to do this. After all, I'm the pastor's wife. It's much more important that I mingle and talk with people.

I expected that I would have to do this in the beginning of our church plant, but when will I get to stop?

Where is Kyle? Why am I solely responsible for the kids on Sundays? Why doesn't he see that I need help? As a matter of fact, he should be doing this, not me.

Fuming by that point, I finished putting everything away and marched the kids to the car. As I helped them into their car seats, Kyle approached the car, stepping right into my crosshairs. I unleashed my frustration on him, not caring who heard me, and drove home sulking and completely miserable.

Sacrifice? What for? All I could think about was myself.

It was not my finest moment.

Unfortunately, I have had too many moments like that in church planting. Not all of them have escalated to that point of frustration or selfishness, but that morning in the parking lot illustrates that my greatest ongoing struggle as a church planting wife has been primarily with myself.

I want to serve God, but only so much. I want to love people, but only those I like. I want to glorify God, but I would like a little glory myself. I'm willing to sacrifice, but only as long as I receive something in return.

My journals capture my conversations with God about my conflicting desires. Less than a month into church planting, already faced with the sacrifice question, I prayed: "Lord, I confess that a rebellious spirit has welled up inside of me. I hate what is going on inside of me: a dissatisfaction with church planting, the thought of *What's in this for me?*, a desire for personal glory instead of doing things to honor You, a complaining spirit about my role, and a lack of desire to help Kyle. This planting thing is taking it out of me, and I long for a life in which I am not asked to sacrifice."

Sadly, my pride surfaced so early.

"People Should Be Serving Me"

Pride displays itself in many forms, but its core is self-elevation:

I don't need anyone; I can take care of myself.

I have rights; I must look out for myself and protect my time, possessions, reputation, and abilities.

I desire to be known as a success and am driven to be known for what I do and how I serve.

I deserve good things.

People should be serving me.

I'm better than others.

I shouldn't have to do anything that I don't want to do or that doesn't benefit me.

It's all about me.

Somewhere I got the idea that ministry automatically affords me perks, respect, followers, and a good reputation. Nancy Leigh DeMoss explains: "The higher up we find ourselves in terms of power, influence, and wealth—the more people who look up to us—the more vulnerable we are to pride and self-deceit, the more prone we are to be blind to our spiritual need and defensiveness. The subtle encroachment of pride is more likely to render us useless to God and others than any other kind of failure."[9]

What does this subtle encroachment of pride look like in the heart of the church planting wife? It is a heart of self-focus: refusing to serve or serving joylessly, remaining aloof from people, resenting our husband, refusing to participate in the life of the church, complaining about the sacrifices required, withholding support from our husband, or desiring to be served and honored.

We often see a similar kind of self-focus in young children.

Our middle son, Reese, loves giving gifts. When there is a birthday to celebrate, he delights in presenting the gift to the person of honor. When he was a preschooler, however, instead of handing the gift to the recipient so they could open it, he often tore into the gift himself. As much as we reminded him that the gift was not for him, that it was meant to bless someone else, that he would enjoy watching the person open his gift, he assumed all parties and presents were about him. When we finally coaxed him to hand over the gift or let the recipient play with the gift, he often pouted or cried. The gift and the blessing of giving were spoiled by his self-focus.

We do the same thing when we make the church plant about us—our comfort, our needs, our desires. Then ministry quickly becomes a burden, and we resist the Lord's calling on our lives, looking for ways out from under that burden. The gift and blessing are spoiled by our self-focus.

When ministry weighs heavy on me, and my heart starts turning away from sacrifice, I hear the echoes of my children's whining in my own complaints to God: "It's too hard. How come so-and-so doesn't have to do this? I want out." Instead of looking for ways to bless others, I become interested in how others can bless me. Rather than seeking ways to affirm others, I seek ways to be affirmed. Instead of sacrificing for the Lord, I expect Him to serve me. My thoughts center on myself: Am I happy? Am I being appreciated? Am I liked? Will someone serve me? Are my needs being met?

From Self-Focus to Self-Denial

The reality is that the ministry of church planting isn't about making us happy and comfortable, and we do not have to give in to our fleshly self-interest or pride. In fact, we do well *not* to give in to them because, in Scripture, God has a strong reaction to self-indulgence. He opposes those who are proud (Proverbs 3:34) and labels spiritual leaders whose hearts are on themselves as hypocrites and vain worshipers (Matthew 15:8–9).

Scripture describes ministry as a sacrificial service unto God.

In 1 Corinthians 4:1, Paul labels himself a servant belonging to Christ. The term refers to a slave who rowed at the bottom of a multilevel ship and who endured falling refuse from others up above. Paul also says being a minister is similar to being a butler or a servant who belongs to another but who is entrusted with managing the household affairs. He models his ministry after Christ, saying, "Imitate me as I also imitate Christ."

What in Christ was Paul imitating?

"Christ Jesus . . . who, though he was in the form of God, did not count equality with God a thing to be grasped, but emptied himself, by taking the form of a servant, being born in the likeness of men. And being found in human form, he humbled himself by becoming obedient to the point of death, even death on a cross" (Philippians 2:6–8 ESV).

Paul's understanding of ministry is that it has nothing to do with accolades or comfort. His focus was not on himself but on others: "[I am] not seeking my own profit, but the profit of many, that they may be saved" (1 Corinthians 10:33). This focus was not only an imitation of Christ's but was also driven and motivated by the love of Christ:

> Scripture's description of ministry certainly stands in stark contrast to my petty thoughts about cleaning up after people.

For if we are beside ourselves, it is for God; or if we are of sound mind, it is for you. For the love of Christ compels us, because we judge thus: that if One died for all, then all died; and He died for all, *that those who live should live no longer for themselves, but for Him who died for them and rose again.* (2 Corinthians 5:13–15)

Paul's ministry focus was on Christ and other people so much that he was willing to endure all manner of hardships: beatings, imprisonment, stoning, shipwrecks, sleepless nights, hunger, nakedness in cold temperatures, false accusations, homelessness, persecution, and defamation. In Colossians 1:24, he described his suffering as a welcome continuation of the Lord's suffering because it allowed him to broadcast the message of the gospel. He aspired to be an in-person representation of Christ, the Suffering Servant.

Scripture's description of ministry certainly stands in stark contrast to my petty thoughts about cleaning up after people. As church planting wives, we will most likely not have to endure the things that Paul did. Our calling, however, is the same: to live for God and for the sake of others, and not for ourselves.

True, we are no longer slaves, but daughters, brought to the table to experience an intimate, familial relationship with God. But our sincere love and gratitude for what Christ has done for us compels us to give up our freedom and stay under the loving ownership of our Father, much like the freed slave described in Exodus 21:5–6: "But if the servant plainly says, 'I love my master, . . . I will not go out free,' then his master shall . . . pierce his ear with an awl; and he shall serve him forever." We are not just servants who perform certain requirements and then go back to our quarters to do what we want. Based on God's love for us and His actions on our behalf, we become willing slaves at His disposal.

How do we get there? How do we move from self-focus to self-denial? For me, the church planting journey alone was enough to draw my pride to the surface. I quickly discovered that I could either allow God to break me or resist the process and be completely miserable. It was the sacrifice question: Will I or won't I?

Church planting will either break you of pride or it will become a significant burden. If you submit to be broken and as you cultivate a humble heart, church planting will become a joy and a blessing. In order to experience the joy and blessing, we must eradicate pride.

Every day.

Be a Learner

One way that pride is defeated is when we understand that church planting is not *about* us but is *for* us. Specifically through church planting, we are on the fast track for growth in faith, character, perseverance, and servanthood. Pride says, "As a church planter and wife, we're swooping in to save the day." A servant says, "I'm here to serve my Master and to learn and grow in the process." Perhaps our growth is the very reason we are where we are, doing what we're doing. As we acknowledge our circumstances as God-ordained opportunities for growth and make ourselves available to Him, pride quickly dissipates.

Helen Roseveare, a missionary in the 1950s and 60s in what is now the Democratic Republic of Congo, illustrates this point using an example from her own life. About her struggles working as a doctor in a hospital full of patients with endless needs, she wrote:

> "Helen," [Jack, a fellow missionary] said quietly. "If you think you have come to the mission field because you are a little better than others, because you have more to offer through your medical training, or—" There was nothing censorious in his tone, yet his words cut deep into my heart. Was that the appearance that I had given to others, of a spiritual superiority, that I knew all the answers and would show them how the job should be done? . . .

Did I subconsciously feel that my service to the community through medicine would bring more people to the Savior than these others had done by years of patient trekking and preaching?

A wave of shame and a sense of failure came over me. I tried not to reply, as a sense of self-pity made itself felt. Why did they misunderstand me? Why did no one appreciate how much I needed fellowship and support? No one offered to help me, or relieve me on night duty. The "pity-poor-little-me" syndrome started early in my missionary career.

"Remember," Jack concluded, "the Lord has only one main purpose ultimately in each of our lives, that is to make us more like our Lord Jesus."

As we talked over the implications of what he was saying, he suggested to me that the next thing God wanted to do in my life to make me more like Jesus, He could not do for me back in Britain, as I was too stubborn and willful: so He had brought me to Africa, to work in me through Africans.

Another voice spoke quite clearly: "To make you realize and face up to this 'pity-poor-little-me' attitude and become real," and I turned my head away.[10]

Many struggles accompany church planting. With what attitude will we respond to our struggles? Pride—a refusal to learn and grow in the struggles or a tendency to blame church planting for the struggles—will only cause us to retreat in self-pity from God and from others. Taking the attitude of a learner, however, will alter the challenges and sacrifices into opportunities for growth.

Take the Mindset of the Master

Second, pride is defeated and a sacrificial heart develops when, like Paul, we imitate our Master. Pride thrives when we decide what we will and won't do or when we are selective about who we will and won't love. The humble servant is not above serving anyone if it means getting to share the love of Christ with others or pleasing God with her faithfulness.

This is what our Master modeled. In the Old Testament, prophets described the coming Messiah as a Suffering Servant who would someday be trampled and abused by men. But because the Jews awaited a figurehead who would conquer and rule over the Romans with power and force, Jesus' style and philosophy completely baffled them. Jesus taught that spiritual leaders were to serve as many people as possible rather than oversee as many people as possible. Jesus didn't look for ways to climb the ladder of power and success, but He consistently sought more ways to minister to the least of these. He rebuked His friends when they fought for honor, saying that the greatest leaders are the ones who serve. Rather than leaving the dirty work for others, He got down on His hands and knees like a lowly servant and wiped the refuse of the world off of His disciples' feet. He ate with sinners. He didn't rush to defend Himself when He was slandered and misunderstood. He healed the outcasts of society with His compassionate touch. He did not come to be served but to serve and to be a ransom for many. And in the process, He turned the world's idea of leadership upside down.

Are we above our Master? Do we think like the Jewish leaders who expected the privileges of leadership yet shunned any of its responsibilities? Our position of influence and leadership does not exclude us from the servant's work. If we follow Christ's example, we will actually seek out opportunities to serve unnoticed. We will not look for others to serve or admire us, nor will we expect comfort and ease in this church planting calling. Instead, we will look to serve and even embrace the sacrifice it requires. Elisabeth Elliot describes Amy Carmichael, a missionary to China, and her attitude toward difficult and seemingly menial work:

> Amy was learning that if the Lord of Glory took a towel and knelt on the floor to wash the dusty feet of His disciples, then no work, even the relentless and often messy routine of caring for squalling babies, is demeaning. To offer it up to the Lord of Glory transforms it into a holy task. "Could it be right," Amy had asked, "to turn from so much that might be of profit [evangelizing] and become just nursemaids?" The answer was yes. *It is not the business of the servant to decide which work is great, which is small, which important*

or unimportant—he is not greater than his master. "If by doing some work which the undiscerning consider 'not spiritual work' I can best help others, and I inwardly rebel, thinking it is the spiritual for which I crave, when in truth it is the interesting and exciting, then I know nothing of Calvary's love," Amy wrote after many years of caring for [children she rescued from child trafficking].[11]

In the church planting world, we tend to think that our service is meaningless unless we have quick numerical growth or accolades to show for it. We assume that God's favor only rests on those planters and wives who are gifted communicators, have dynamic personalities, or keep coming up with innovative ideas. We discount the daily acts of obedience and faith such as having the neighbors over for dinner, pursuing relationships with unbelievers, counseling a distraught church member, setting up for church, or starting a moms' group. However, the servant does the unseen or the small, trusting that God can produce fruit from it. The servant knows it is for Him anyway; He can do with it what He chooses.

> Most of the time, I am eager and willing to join in the work of the church.

Having a servant's heart doesn't mean that we take responsibility for every need, but it does mean that our hearts will be attuned to the direction of the Master. It means that we are *willing*—willing to serve the person we don't like, to say yes when our husbands ask for our help, to go out of our way for someone else—all for the sake of Christ.

This understanding, that our service as a church planting wife is ultimately for Christ, lays the final death blow to our pride.

I have tried to excuse myself from serving based on the idea that this is my husband's calling alone. Most of the time, I am eager and willing to join in the work of the church, to give of my time and home to people, and to free my husband up to do what he has been called to do. But sometimes the demands and the sacrifices seem too much. On those days, I feel needy for my husband's time and attention. I want to get off the merry-go-round for a moment. I wish my husband's work was a 9 to 5 job. I want to step out from his shadow for a little bit. I want my own way.

In my self-pity, I recall all the times that I have been literally shoved aside by someone wanting to get to my husband, or how I have given up so much of myself to help my husband be successful. It seems to me, as I look through this filter, that I have sacrificed so much for *him*. All the self-pity turns to selfishness as I start counting all the things I deserve. I'd love to have acclaim from others, time off, my husband's appreciation, and on and on.

Not Just a Tagalong

The fact of it is that the Lord called me to ministry just as He did my husband. It's not as if He called Kyle and I'm just a tagalong through his life. It's just that my ministry looks different. My ministry is often in the background, praying for my husband, encouraging him when he's discouraged, and being a sounding board for him. My ministry also involves training our children and providing a warm, loving home environment for our family. And then, beyond my relationship with God and my ministry to my family, God has given me a ministry to our church through discipleship and hospitality. So while my husband is leading, teaching, counseling, decision making, and vision casting—a very visible ministry—I am generally serving behind the scenes.

This is a sacrifice, no doubt about it. This type of ministry largely goes unnoticed and can, on those self-pity days, seem purposeless and of little value. But is it? We often categorize service or spiritual gifts according to what we value or admire, but God is not impressed by what we are impressed by. He values faithfulness, whether it's seen or unseen by human eyes, and ultimately, my service is for Him anyway. Although I love my family and my church, I don't do these things for them but for the Lord. If I attempt to do things in order to please people, I will be miserable. But if I work diligently in ministry for the eyes of God and to bring honor to God, knowing He sees and He will reward, I do well, and I enjoy getting to be a part of God's activity. When I consider how He has sacrificed for me, my sacrifice suddenly seems so small.

Remember that church planting is not just your husband's calling, it is yours as well. You may not have been thrilled about church planting, and you may have come into it with many fears, but you can know for certain that if God has called your husband to plant, He has called you, too. You may be serving people and helping your husband, but, as you do these things, you're really doing them for the Lord. Knowing and acting on that knowledge will motivate you to serve the "least of these" with joy rather than demanding your rights.

Sacrifice *Will* Be Rewarded

Jesus said that if we follow Him, we are like dead people because we have been crucified with Him: "If anyone would come after me, he must deny himself and take up his cross daily and follow me" (Luke 9:23 NIV). In biblical times, a cross was an instrument of death, only carried by those with a death sentence. The death Jesus describes means we resist self-lordship, abandon all our earthly hopes, plans, and ambitions, and take up His ambitions for us. We invest all we are and have in the Lord. We are dead to our lives before Christ but alive through Christ unto God.

We often live, however, as if we are dead to Christ and alive to ourselves. Our flesh, attempting to dethrone God, tries to deceive us, by telling us that life could never be found in sacrificial death.

We tend to take offense at the idea that, as church planting wives, our calling is to lay down our rights and give ourselves for the sake of others, especially those who don't appreciate or understand our sacrifice for them. Although releasing control over our lives and living for the sake of others seems antithetical to our happiness, it is very much for our joy. Just after Jesus says that His followers must deny themselves, He tells them why: "For whoever wants to save his life will lose it, but whoever loses his life for me will save it" (Luke 9:24 NIV). While pride leads to misery and downfall, sacrifice is the very foundation of an abundant life. Consider what Paul—the one who suffered immensely for the sake of the gospel—says about denying himself:

> In everything I did, I showed you by this hard work we must help the weak, remembering the words the Lord Jesus himself said: "**It is more blessed to give than to receive.**" (Acts 20:35 NIV)

> **Now I rejoice in what was suffered for you,** and I fill up in my

flesh what is still lacking in regard to Christ's afflictions, for the sake of his body, which is the church. I have become its servant by the commission God gave me to present to you the word of God in its fullness. (Colossians 1:24–25 NIV)

Blessed are the poor in spirit [the nonprideful]. (Matthew 5:3 NIV)

Sacrifice results in our joy.

It is also rewarded.

Just a few months into our church plant, my husband left for a week to lead a missions training conference for college ministers. It was difficult for me to joyfully let him go, knowing I would be at home by myself with three small children. He went, and God used him there, but I felt a nagging sense that my sacrifice was measly next to the work he had done for the Lord that week. Soon after, however, I received a letter from the president of the mission organization who had planned the conference. In it, he reminded me that my sacrifice, seemingly small, was valuable to the Lord. He wrote:

My wife and I want to tell you a story and in so doing express our deep gratitude for the role you have played in God's using men and women to help fulfill His purposes. We do not take your sacrifice lightly or for granted.

My wife is not an adventurous soul and because we still had children at home when we started [the organization], she was unable to travel with me. It was a difficult time for us, but God's hand and shared calling on us was clear. There were going to be times that I would have to be away from home. She so wanted to be part of what God was doing and really didn't understand how she might do that until she read a story about King David and his army in 1 Samuel 30:3–4, 17–24. David and his army of 600 were returning home from war. They were exhausted and discouraged.

"When David and his men came to Ziklag, they found it destroyed by fire and their wives and sons and daughters had been taken captive . . .

Then David came to the 200 men who had been too exhausted

to follow him and who were left behind at the Besor Ravine. They came out to meet David and the people with him. As David and his men approached, he greeted them. But all the evil men and troublemakers among David's followers said, 'Because they did not go out with us, we will not share with them the plunder we recovered.'"

David's response to these evil men has been a tremendous encouragement to my wife through the years when she has been unable to travel with me.

"David replied, 'No, my brothers, you must not do that with what the Lord has given us. He has protected us and handed over to us the forces that came against us. Who will listen to what you say? *The share of the man who stayed with the supplies is to be the same as that of him who went down to the battle. All will share alike.'"*

My wife and I want to express our deep gratitude to you for your role in what God did in the lives of students this week. Your willingness to stay home (stay with the supplies) helped to make the week a great success. Young men and women walk more closely with God because of the sacrifice you made. You share in that equally with all of us.

The Lord sees our sacrifice and is pleased with it. It is for Him, and He is revealed in us when we deny ourselves and live for Him. A prideful heart is vanity, as fleeting as the wind, but the sacrifices of a servant's heart are never in vain:

Therefore, my dear [sisters], stand firm. Let nothing move you. Always give yourselves fully to the work of the Lord, because you know that your labor in the Lord is not in vain. (1 Corinthians 15:58 NIV)

I have a grievance speech packed away in my heart that I pull out and start to unpack at least once a month. It's never said to a soul but said to God, so that I can once again hash out with Him why we are church planting, and if He is really using me in it. He always brings me back to the realization that this is not a burden but a privilege, and that, when it is done with a sacrificial heart, it is certainly not an easy life, but it is a purposeful, meaningful, God-honoring life.

I'm learning to find joy in sacrifice.

What about you?

Cultivating Your Heart

Can you identify with these statements from the chapter?

- Pride says, "As a church planter and wife, we're swooping in to save the day." A servant says, "I'm here to serve my Master and to learn and grow in the process."

- I want to serve God, but only so much. I want to love people, but only those I like. I want to glorify God, but I would like a little glory myself. I'm willing to sacrifice, but only as long as I receive something in return.

Are there days or even seasons when you struggle with the sacrifices you're making as a church planting wife? What are these challenges? Be as specific as you can.

How can you move willingly and joyfully from self-focus to self-denial? Identify areas in which you have already found victory (or at least made progress!).

Interview with

Ginger Vassar

Ginger's husband, JR, is the pastor of Apostles Church in New York City. Together, they planted the church on Manhattan in 2005 in their living room. The church began with thirteen people, has seen steady growth since its inception, and now meets in two areas of Manhattan. Ginger and JR have three children.

There is so much sacrifice required of church planting wives because of their husband's job. Have you ever struggled with resentment about that, and how have you battled against it?

We all deal with resentment. Let's be honest, our hearts are prone to wander in that direction, whether it's over church, kids, housework, a pet peeve, really anything. I think one of the best ways to battle resentment is learning to be content. Where is your heart? your "center"? If it is wrapped up in people's approval, recognition over your tasks done well, even your faithfulness as a wife to leave comforts of "home" to move and plant somewhere, then you will feel entitled to some pats on the back or at least a desire for some help with the load you bear.

We do bear a large load, especially if we are moving to an unfamiliar place with a family. We will bear the brunt of finding grocery stores, post office, libraries, playgrounds, schools, and even trying, along with our kids, to make new friends. It's taxing. We are making a new life, sometimes in a distant place or one that has a different set of values than we have within our homes. It is easy to elevate the "sacrifice" we have made for the sake of the gospel and seek reward in the "here and now." Jesus modeled that sometimes we won't get our reward until we hear Him say, "Well done." Sacrifice should not come as a surprise to believers; remember that Jesus walked that road fully and more deeply than we can know.

Another way to battle resentment is with perseverance. I love to read Hebrews because the message to believers is to press on. Persevering wouldn't be persevering without a certain degree of difficulty. "Let us cling to Jesus and never stop trusting him" (see Hebrews 4:14–16). He is our perfect

High Priest—one who has been there persevering to the end and able to relate to any and every struggle we face. Galatians 6:9 has been huge to me: "Let us not grow weary in doing good for at the right time you will see a harvest" (my paraphrase).

One more thing that comes to mind is humility. Philippians 2:3–4 (ESV) has become a motto in our home in how we treat each other and those outside our home. Our attitude should be like Jesus': "Do nothing from rivalry or conceit, but in humility count others more significant than yourself . . . look out . . . for the interests of others." You can't praise your own efforts, triumphs, or even your sacrifices and be humble. Jesus sees, and in that we must rest. He is for me so that I can be for others, whether I am recognized or not.

What has been your greatest personal struggle(s) in church planting and what have you learned that might benefit another church planting wife?

My struggle early on was my desire to be praised for what I had started or done. I ran our kids' ministry for a couple of years. My prideful desire for recognition over all of my "hard work" week in and week out led me to harbor bitterness toward volunteers when they did not use some element of a lesson that I spent a lot of time on. The problem was not in them, it was in me, in my heart. I had to deal with that bitterness before the Lord! Church planting is so revealing. It flings wide open the heavy curtains we shade those aspects of selfishness and pride with. Sanctification on steroids!

What advice would you give a church planting wife just starting out?

You and your husband have to be on the same team. I know that sounds simplistic, but it is right on. Be in tune to each other's personal needs. You two are the only ones who will recognize your own personal needs. Lean on each other, have healthy communication, be extra intuitive at building each other up. Protect time together and family time as much as possible. Keep your marriage free from being the thing that weighs you down. You are laying your life down for the church, but your home is the starting block for a healthy outlook on ministry. It's easy to pour your efforts into the church, but make sure you aren't neglecting the family God gave you and the marriage He blessed you with. Let your husband lead and praise his leadership. Involve children where appropriate, but don't load them down with the same calling that you and your husband carry. They are still learning by your lead, and you are to gently lead and teach them. Model in your home what you are trying to do in your city. Keep the central message of your home the gospel. Pray for your children to see and love Jesus and that your children would learn to show the love of Jesus. Isn't that, simply put, what we are doing in our city as planters?

CHAPTER SIX

the Faithful Heart

FORSAKING FEAR

D o you remember where you were or what you were doing when God called you to join Him in the adventure of church planting? I remember my own calling in several distinct, memorable mental snapshots.

Clear Focus

Snapshot #1: In my mind's eye, I am sitting in the back of a large church sanctuary. There is activity at the front by the stage—people and music and commotion—but the low lights have insulated me from others and created intimacy between the Lord and me. I am praying silently and earnestly, crying out to God for change. My heart, so restless and weary, grows still as I recognize the overwhelming presence of God and sense the importance of the moment. In my expectancy, my mind is clear and, although God doesn't give me instructions or direction, I know I have been heard. He has plans in the works. My heart floods with peace and relief.

Snapshot #2: Two years later, sitting in the back of a room, I am listening to Kyle as he exhorts a group of ministry leaders to be strong and courageous using the biblical example of Joshua and Caleb. Despite their circumstances and the obstacles they faced, he says, Joshua and Caleb believed God would give them the land He had promised them. I am intensely and suddenly aware that God is speaking directly to me, to us. Clearly, we will soon be asked to look beyond our circumstances with eyes of faith and believe God will give us a specific land. As I furiously take notes, trying to capture the moment, I feel like a runner stepping into the starting blocks but who is unable to see a clear finish line.

Snapshot #3: A few months after Kyle's Joshua and Caleb talk, I am at home preparing dinner when Kyle arrives, talking excitedly about a conversation he had with a church planter that morning. Kyle said, "He asked if I have ever considered church planting." *Strange*, I thought. This man is the second church planter in a few weeks' time to broach the subject with Kyle. Church planting fits so neatly with what the Joshua and Caleb talk ignited in my heart. Over dinner, we agree that church planting is something we must prayerfully consider. Something about the idea sits right in my soul, a heightened awareness that God is bringing finality to all of our questions and uncertainties. After Kyle's conversations with church planting pastors and our dinner discussion, we decide to attend a church planting conference, at which God clearly confirms our calling to church plant.

Snapshot #4: I'm at the back of a room full of college students, watching a video of faces and cultural landmarks from around the world. We have just returned from a discovery trip to Charlottesville with one prayer: "Lord, show us if this is what You want us to do and if this is where You want us to go." The lights are low, and the darkness envelopes me in a warm cocoon. Because Kyle is a college and missions pastor, I have seen this type of video many times before. But this time, as I watch the faces flicker on the screen, a feeling of urgency floods my body. I am aware that the video is meant for me. I am to go. I am to be a part of God's unfolding story. Now is the time. Church planting is the call. Charlottesville is the place. I am overwhelmingly excited at the prospect.

Remember

What about you? What are your snapshots? How did God make your calling clear?

Maybe it was fast and furious, apparent in one moment. Perhaps it unfolded over a period of time, like it did for me. Or maybe it was more like my friend Shauna, who was relaxing in the bathtub when her husband sprung the church planting idea on her out of nowhere. She prayerfully wrestled with the idea for ten days before God confirmed the calling, and she enthusiastically agreed.

As you think about your own mental snapshots, consider this: What did you know for sure at those moments? Did you know where you would live or where your financial support would come from? Did you know who would be in your core group? Did you know the names or faces of neighbors, coworkers, or friends you would love and serve? Did you know what the church would look like or how it would grow? Did you know what the first year or two of the church's existence would be like? Did you know the outcome from the beginning? Most likely, you knew nothing at all except a general sense of the calling to church plant.

That was then. What is now? Is there a difference between that day and now?

And you said yes.

It may have been a shout or a fearful whisper, but you said yes to God. Your yes was an act of faith because, after all, faith is the substance of things hoped for, the evidence of things not seen (Hebrews 11:1). When you offered your yes to God and your support to your husband, there were literally hundreds of unseen things before you. Only faith flies into the unseen like that.

Now consider how you felt when you said yes. Although you did not know details or steps or outcomes or results, you likely felt peace, joy, and certainty about God's leadership and future provision. Certainly, fear threatened to crash the party, but your big faith turned fear and doubt away at the door. God gave you an invitation to faith and you accepted. You were gung ho, ready to go, and pumped full with spiritual adrenaline.

That was then.

What is now?

Is there a difference between that day and now?

Whether you are still preparing to plant the church or you have been planting for several years, I imagine that if you are like me, at some point your faith has wavered, giving way to anxiety or fear. The mental snapshots have grown fuzzy, the details of the calling less clear.

Most people express amazement at our initial willingness to follow God into the unknown of church planting. It does take great faith. But, as we know all too well, starting something is easier (and more exciting) than the daily, sustaining faith it takes to grow a church. In my experience, the first steps of faith were easier compared to the everyday, one- or two-years-later kind of faith.

I am so thankful that I recorded my mental snapshots in a journal because those crisp, clear pictures of God's calling have faded with time and hardships. I must recall them constantly. *Remember God's promises. Remember what He has done. Consider His faithfulness.* I have discovered that if I don't remember the clarity with which He spoke or His faithfulness along the way, certainty and peace so easily and quickly give way to doubt and unrest. In my fear, I lose sight of Him and His bigger-picture purposes for us.

Sometimes I have longed for the unwavering faith I had at the beginning. I miss the big-splash, celebrated faith. I wonder where that woman went, the immoveable, crazy-faith one. Why, even after all I've seen and experienced, am I now undone by silly, trivial fears or plagued by doubt?

A Continuing Faith

My tendency is to try living off of my onetime, big-step faith instead of cultivating a daily trust of and dependence on God. In our first year, I treated church planting as a onetime event and then faced the day-to-day discouragements or hardships with trepidation and self-reliance. Sadly, I doubted that the same God who called us would actually help us fulfill the calling, so I determined that the work was up to my husband and me. I tried working myself out of fear.

Paul speaks to this tendency as it concerns salvation and sanctification: "Did you receive the Spirit by the works of the law, or by the hearing of faith? Are you so foolish? Having begun in the Spirit, are you now being made perfect by the flesh? . . . Therefore He who supplies the Spirit to you and works miracles among you, does He do it by the works of the law, or by the hearing of faith?" (Galatians 3:2-3, 5). The Galatians started well—by faith—but followed up their initial act of saving faith with try-hard, pull-up-by-the-bootstraps attempts at spiritual growth.

Just because our church is starting to get its legs or got its legs a long time ago doesn't mean that we no longer walk by faith. Church planting requires faith at the beginning, in the middle, and, in fact, faith all the way through. It requires trusting God for the initial provision—financial support, direction, and a core group—but it also requires trusting Him for the ongoing provision of numerical growth, spiritual growth, networks, encouragement, financial support, favor, wisdom, fruitfulness, and heart change.

I thought we'd have a difficult climb up the mountain, and then we would get to the top and everything would be easy from there. We would feel like insiders in our city, the church would grow like crazy and have no problems, people would love and respect us and let us into their lives. While we do feel like we're making inroads, meeting people, growing, and connecting, the work is not getting any easier. In fact, church planting is getting more difficult as the church grows. The brighter the light in a very dark place, the more we attract the fiery arrows of the enemy.

> When I think about how this adventure of faith has completely changed my worldview, I am overcome with joy at the privilege I have been given.

Again and again, the Lord takes me to Hebrews 10-12 and reminds me that this calling (and the Christian life) is one of faith, *everyday* faith. Faith means we live for something that is still to come, for joy here and an eternal reward. It means we may never see the results of our hard work. It means that we acknowledge our weakness and poverty so that Christ can be strong in us. God's concern is less about our circumstances, ministries, or activities, and more about our faith *through* them.

I often want a Hebrews 10–12 life that doesn't require faith and where the rewards and results are immediate, but these chapters instead illustrate faith through the lives of believers who were willing to endure anything on earth for the sake of Christ and for their eternal rewards. In light of those who lived so faithfully before us, we must throw off the weight of fear and sin of self-reliance and run with marathon endurance toward Jesus—the Finish Line, the Goal, the Reward. Faith is both the fuel for our race and the final victory.

Certainly, church planting has been difficult and discouraging at many points along the way. There have been days when fear has gotten the best of me, when I have wanted to give up and go "home," or when I have been bitter about the calling God has placed on our lives. But when I think about all the things I have seen God do—literally making something out of nothing—and how this adventure of faith has completely changed my worldview, I am overcome with joy at the privilege I have been given. A life that requires trusting God is an abundant life.

Church planting has made my faith stronger and more certain, because I've gone out on a limb with God, and He's been faithful.

On the Limb

Once you go out on a limb with God and see with your own eyes who He is and what He can do, there is nothing that He asks of you that you won't do. When we fight to stay in certain and controlled circumstances, seek comfort over discomfort, or need a fully mapped-out plan, can we even claim faith in God at all?

This is why we must *continue* to go out on a limb with God as much as He gives us opportunity to do so, which in church planting is almost every day. We must seek new perspectives, learn our new culture, cultivate relationships with people unlike us, and listen to the God-stirrings in our hearts. We must initiate spiritual conversations, purposefully place ourselves in situations where we don't know outcomes or answers, try things that might fail, and allow discomfort. We must be curious, hear people's stories, consider others more important than ourselves, face challenges head-on, attempt things that may seem silly to other people, and observe the world and where God is moving in it. We must move from one spot to another. We must look fear in the face, unblinking and unmoved.

Because when we go out on a limb with God, the safety harnesses cannot go, too.

Because when we go out on a limb with God, we cannot rely on our own cunning, skill, or plan.

> Surprisingly, we also learn to love being out on the limb.

Because when we go out on a limb with God, we have *only Him*. This, I think, He relishes. He waits for. He throws His hands up in exaltation because here—out on the limb—He gets to be God as He wants to be: faithful and true, gentle and gracious, bold and wise, powerful and capable.

With all safety harnesses gone, He speeds our spiritual growth, knowing that we have nothing else to cling to other than Him. There, in that fragile spot, we learn to depend on Him.

There, surprisingly, we also learn to love being out on the limb.

Because He is there. And, because He is, we learn that we have nothing to be afraid of.

Thankfully, in church planting we have plenty of opportunities to go out on a limb with God. Standing on faith rather than fear is really *the* test of church planting. So even though you have already said *Yes, God*, even though you believed Him for the church plant, even though you stepped out onto the limb in a burst of spiritual adrenaline, do not let your faith be a past faith. Let each day be a renewal of faith, another opportunity to say yes to God.

The Faith of Those Who Went Before

When I am fearful and doubting God's provision, I return not only to my snapshots but to the stories of faithful people recorded in Scripture. I often revisit Sarah's story: Sarah, the mother of all church planting wives.

We all know the story, but we often think of it as Abraham's story. God told Abraham to drop everything and go, but He didn't give him any other details except a promise about the future and a promise of His presence. He said: "Leave your country, your people and your father's household and go to the land I will show you. I will make you into a great nation and I will bless you; I will make your name great, and you will be a blessing. I will bless those who bless you, and whoever curses you I will curse; and all peoples on earth will be blessed through you" (Genesis 12:1–3 NIV).

When God finishes speaking with Abraham, the story becomes Sarah's, too. I imagine that when Abraham got home that evening, he sat Sarah down and solemnly announced what God had asked of him. As any wife would do, Sarah likely began asking questions: "Where is our final destination? And why are we going? Have you thought this through? Are you sure you heard correctly? This just doesn't add up." Abraham didn't have the answers. He didn't know the end of the story, what God specifically had in mind for them, or the specific outcome of this seemingly dramatic move. He only had the promise of a coming child.

And she went. She followed her husband and her God into the great unknown. She left her home, her family, and the familiarity of her culture. We know somewhat how that feels despite our ability to stay connected to family through technology—a rush of adventure and fear all mixed up together.

Sarah was probably just like us: imagining the ideal, expecting immediate results, and never for once considering what adversity might come before God fulfilled His promise. A few weeks in, she likely began the pregnancy tests, anticipating the moment when she shared the positive result with Abraham.

They Feared

Soon however, Abraham and Sarah faced their first obstacle, and small cracks begin showing in their faith. Instead of staying in Canaan and trusting God to provide, famine led them on a side trip to Egypt, and Abraham, out of fear, asked Sarah to act as his sister rather than his wife. Sarah agreed, perhaps wanting to believe that God meant to fulfill His promise through the pharaoh or, more likely, because Abraham had transferred his fears to her.

This is what fear does: it causes us to question the specifics of the original promise, diverts our attention and energy away from where God has us, and spreads like a contagion.

For Abraham and Sarah, fear arose because they started believing that the promise was simply impossible. They began looking at their situation with physical eyes, calculating with logical, analytical formulas to see how it could possibly happen. They no longer saw the promise through the spiritual lens of God's power and authority but only through their circumstances.

I've had days when I have looked at my church planting life through a rational, logical lens and completely panicked. What have we done? How did we get here? Is this working? How are we going to provide for ourselves? Have we been silly or irrational to think we could actually plant a church? I start frantically mapping out our plan B. Worse, my fear transfers easily to my husband. Expressing my worries, I pull his attention away from God's promises to us and cause him to grow discouraged.

Fear arises when we look at our circumstances rather than looking at God, when we look at what is right in front of us with our human eyes. We may feebly acknowledge that God is able, but our faith wavers and weakens, and we doubt our original calling. Fear paralyzes us from moving forward or, like with Sarah, urges us to take matters into our own hands.

They Took Control

A full yet empty ten years later, Sarah is still waiting. *Ten years.* In modern day church planting terms, that's a whole lot of setting up chairs for people who never materialize, a lot of effort with nothing to show for it, a lot of discouragement, and a lot of talk of giving up and going home.

To make matters worse, fear had come to reside in Sarah's home in the form of a maidservant, Hagar. Hagar should never have been part of the equation because Abraham should never have led them into Egypt, just as Abraham should never have convinced Sarah to act as his sister. And all of these acts of disobedience culminated into one disastrous choice: Sarah's decision to try plan B.

Sarah went to Abraham with an idea: to produce the promise

herself through her husband and her maidservant. Tired of waiting for God, fearful that God might not actually do it, she decided to solve the problem in a way that seemed right to her. Her idea was culturally acceptable, a *natural* answer. She took full control of the situation and tried to force God's hand.

Fear results in anxiety. Anxiety begs us to take control, create our own outcomes, come up with alternate plans. We don't believe God is going to come through for us, so we must come through for ourselves. We lie awake at night sorting ideas, making lists, and creating plans. We try hard to make this church thing come together or we badger our husband to *do this* or *do that,* never at peace or at rest until we are satisfied that everything is under control. And when things don't go how we imagined, when our efforts to control end up hurting our husbands or our families or ourselves, we cast all the blame on our husbands or our God.

That's what Sarah did. When Hagar had a child, Sarah grew bitter and blamed Abraham for her misery. In reality, Sarah's fearful disobedience resulted in her own difficulties. Instead of birthing a child, she birthed her own insecurities.

I understand Sarah's insecurities. When we visited Charlottesville for the first time, other Virginia pastors consistently spoke of the city as a spiritually dark place. *There is something about Charlottesville,* they all said. I sensed that they were secretly glad they were not called to pastor in Charlottesville and fearful for us. As we toured the city, experienced its unique culture, and met students attending the elite University of Virginia, I cowered. These people were too smart, too cultured, too different from us. We could never reach them. We didn't belong in Charlottesville. God could use others, but not us. Our gifts and personalities are not right for this.

Maybe I am not cut out to be a church planting wife.

I would learn that it had nothing to do with me but everything to do with God and His purposes.

Sarah learned that, too. Thirteen years after Ishmael was born, God came to Abraham again. He altered their names, signaling a renewed relationship with them, and, as the Lord spoke with Abraham, Sarah stood just outside the tent door, listening as God said she would finally become a mother. After all this time, after all the steps and missteps, Sarah would see the promise fulfilled. She simply laughed.

Through it all—the side trip to Egypt, the falsehoods, the child through the maidservant—God carried out His plan. His promise could never be fulfilled by human efforts or natural circumstances, nor altered by fear or deceit. He always proves Himself to be God. His words to Sarah illustrate what He desires most from her and from us: "Is anything too hard for the Lord?" Faith. He wants our faith.

Cultivating Faith

When I am fearful and doubting, I think of Sarah's story because it shows God is faithful and that His plans cannot be thwarted by my insecurities and ineptitudes. I am so much like her, and God is still the same God. Sarah was not perfect in her faith, but, in the end, God called her faithful. In fact, Peter spoke prophetically to church planting wives from Sarah's life: "You are [Sarah's] daughters if you . . . do not give way to fear" (1 Peter 3:6 NIV).

How can we cultivate faith and become a daughter of Sarah?

The Heart Sits Down

Abraham and Sarah's faith rested on God.

"Against all hope, Abraham in hope believed and so became the father of many nations, just as it had been said to him, 'So shall your offspring be.' Without weakening in his faith, he faced the fact that his body was as good as dead—since he was about a hundred years old— and that Sarah's womb was also dead. Yet he did not waver through unbelief regarding the promise of God, but was strengthened in his faith and gave glory to God" (Romans 4:18-20 NIV).

This passage doesn't say Abraham agreed with the theological understanding of God or mentally assented to the existence of God. Those beliefs are right and good, but faith comes only when we cling in trust to the *Person* of God. Fearless faith comes when we believe God to be the One who gives life to the dead and calls things that are not as though they were. Abraham was "fully persuaded that God had power to do what he had promised" (NIV). The more we know God and the more we know His character, the more we can depend on Him and the more we can trust Him.

I once heard that a people group in Ecuador define peace as the "heart sitting down," and that is just what happens in my soul when I think about the unchanging character of God. All the worries darting through my mind, all the weight of my sin, all the burdens of motherhood and ministry fall right off in light of these truths. My heart sits down, at peace.

There is hope *always* because this Person at the core of the gospel is unchanging. Because of this, these truths about Him are everlasting.

This has so much to do with my everyday life as a disciple, mother, and church planting wife because the only sure thing I know is change. Any fear or worry I have stems from knowing that life can look drastically different from one day to the next. I am frail and unknowing; I cannot predict or control tomorrow. My attempts to resist change or even to get a firm grasp on today are like trying to cup the wind in my hands.

Sometimes we believe that security comes in change—a new house, different job, change in marital status—and sometimes we believe security comes in hiding or running from change. But security only comes in the unchangeable One, even as the stuff of life is being constantly reworked.

He is the only sure thing, even more certain than the sun rising and the seasons changing, even more certain than the most secure relationships, even more certain than life and death. When we realize this, we can let go of our death grip on life, stop fearing the future, and enjoy the adventure of life because we are hidden safely in the unchangeable One.

Our hearts can sit down.

Regard God's Promises

Abraham and Sarah not only regarded the person of God, but they also regarded the promises of God. I imagine they repeated them to each other often during the many hours of travel. What did they talk about in the many years of barrenness *after* the promise was given? What did they discuss after Abraham went off course with Hagar?

Certainly he and Sarah were tempted to waver in their faith again or doubt that God would fulfill His promise to them. We know in the end that Abraham was declared righteous by God; therefore they must have regarded God's promises often, maybe daily or hourly repeating them to each other.

If we are to have a strong faith, we also must regard the promises of God. Sarah had one promise, but we have a multitude recorded for us in Scripture. When we know God and know His promises, we are better equipped to exercise our faith. And just as our muscles become stronger as we work them, our faith muscles are also strengthened and emboldened the more we work them. When our faith is strong, we spend less time battling fear and insecurity and more time carrying out God's calling on our lives. We are also more willing to do difficult or uncomfortable things.

Look through Spiritual Eyes

Sarah could have looked at her circumstances and given up, but she eventually learned to look beyond them with spiritual eyes and see the possible in the impossible. She probably couldn't imagine how God was going to fulfill His promise, but she watched and waited, strengthening her faith and giving thanks to God for His provision in the process.

Charlottesville is a beautiful place to live, but it is not somewhere I would be unless God had given me spiritual eyes for this place. Looking through spiritual eyes at this city and the people I've met gives me a glimpse of God's perspective and purpose for me and for this community. I believe He can do what appears impossible in this city.

Ask God to give you eyes of faith for your city and your church. Ask Him to show you that He planted you there on purpose and for a purpose. Wait expectantly for what is to come and acknowledge the milestones of God's provision.

Spread Faith

Like Sarah to Abraham, we as church planting wives also have many opportunities to offer our assessment of a situation to our husbands, our children, family members, and other women. Will we speak of God's faithfulness and capability, or will we spread fear and anxiety? When our husbands struggle with fear, will we feed it, or will we urge them on with a reminder of God's faithfulness? When other women question whether they can obey God, will you feed their fears or proclaim God's goodness? Your faith breeds faith in your husband, your children, the church, and your community. Through your unwavering faith, you have great influence because, as you champion and believe God, others will, too.

Prepare for Joy

When Abraham and Sarah were called to go, they went, not knowing where they were going or why. Through their everyday faith, they have blessed generations of people. Sarah could never have known what God planned to do through her family, but still, she believed and obeyed.

Sarah had faith because her eyes were on the prize—the pleasure of God.

I recently read an article about a missionary family living in East Africa. They are the first missionaries in their region since the early 1900s, a time when the natives butchered missionaries with machetes. The family works among tribal peoples and is regularly threatened by lions. At the end of the article, the dad said, "Any discomfort pales in comparison to the importance of the task. God is truly faithful. I've gotten more by being here than I have ever given. . . . I hope that other believers will consider a call to missions and make sure they do not live their lives as spiritual cowards."[12]

That last part struck me. Like these missionaries, I want to tell my story about how I've seen God do amazing things just because I believed Him. About how, if we are not doing things that require faith, we are not being used by God and we're not *truly* experiencing God. We are missing out on His great plan of blessing us so that we can be a blessing to others.

When the child of promise was born, Sarah laughed again—this time from joy. She said, "God has made me laugh, and all who hear will laugh with me" (Genesis 21:6). Sarah's life illustrates that faith in God breeds joy. May our lives illustrate the same.

When I sat silently in that cavernous sanctuary feeling God's peace fall on me and when I stood at the stove listening to Kyle say the words "church planting," I didn't have any understanding of what God had in store for us. I did not know any specifics of where we would live, how we would support ourselves, or what the first years of church planting would be like. The outcomes were unclear, but, just like you, we said yes to God's calling on our lives without knowing any of the details. If I had tried visualizing our future, I couldn't have imagined what the reality of this adventure would be.

But now I have new, corresponding mental snapshots, altars in my mind where I have stopped to reflect on what God has done and how He has been faithful.

In an elementary school gym, I am preparing to take communion. I am standing at the end of a long line, my eyes moving from face to face and my heart thanking God for each person He has brought into our lives. *How did this happen? How did we get to this point?* I ask myself. I am overwhelmed by God's grace and faithfulness.

Kyle and I are sitting across from a young couple at our kitchen table. After praying and yearning for a worship leader, we are finally looking at him. We have actually known these two for years since they were students in our college ministry in Texas. We could never have guessed that we would serve or do life with them again, and we are so grateful. God has graciously and faithfully provided for all of us.

I am talking with a young woman I have been discipling. A year before, she was doubting her salvation and entangled in fear. Now, as we are ending our discipleship relationship, she asks me questions about the discipleship relationship she has started with another girl in our church. At the recognition that she is leading, serving, and reproducing her faith in someone else, joy fills my heart. God is faithfully implanting discipleship into the culture of our church.

My new mental snapshots are the tangible certainties that answer all the questions I had in the beginning of this church planting adventure. The difference between those first days and now is that my faith has been stretched bigger, *much* bigger. I have seen God take the vision He gave us and make it come true, even imparting that vision into the people in our church. They have become mirrors reflecting God's faithfulness back to us. God continues to call me forward, to believe Him in new ways, to abandon my fears and depend on Him.

And I say *yes*.

Cultivating Your Heart

The more we know God and the more we know His character, the more we can depend on Him and trust Him. When we turn to Him with our fears and doubts, we find Him to be trustworthy. Consider what the following verses tell us about His character:

Psalm 102:25–27
Psalm 139:7–10
Job 9:4
1 Thessalonians 5:24
Psalm 100:5
1 John 4:8–10
Genesis 18:14
Deuteronomy 32:4

God has made general promises about what He will do for you, His child:

He will not leave you. Ever. (Matthew 28:20)
He protects you from the Evil One. (2 Thessalonians 3:3)
He has given you a Helper. (John 16:7)
He has gifted you to serve Him. (Romans 12:5–8)
He gives you strength and power when you are weary. (Isaiah 40:29)
He teaches and guides you. (Psalm 25:8–10)
He meets your needs. (Philippians 4:19)

Thankfully, God's promises are not impersonal, blanket statements. They are not just for Abraham, Sarah, and other spiritual giants. They are for you and me, and we must cling to them, memorize them, speak them to ourselves, and let them infiltrate and dictate our thoughts and emotions.

If you haven't already done so, consider the specific ways that He has already kept His promises to you. Remembering God's faithfulness will help you exercise your faith going forward.

Interview with

Lora
Batterson

Mark and Lora Batterson planted National Community Church in Washington, D. C. in 1996. NCC is having an impact on D. C. through ten weekly services at six locations and through Ebenezers Coffeehouse, from which all profits go to community outreach projects. Lora and Mark have three children.

Long before planting National Community Church, you and your husband attempted a plant in the Chicago area that never got off the ground. Many church planting wives experience the same thing: implosions of core groups, a church that isn't growing, churches that seem to not be working. What did you learn through that failed church plant experience that you could offer as encouragement to wives who are discouraged or struggling?

I think we were young enough at the time to say, "Okay, what's next?" We were putting one foot in front of the other, trying to discover what great thing we could do for God. But in time, we learned it was all about God using circumstances to conform us to His image. It has to be the right place, the right time, and the right person. If all of those don't align, then sometimes the dream has to die and be resurrected in different circumstances or at a different time. Sometimes God has something better.

Along the same lines, we believe as church planters that God calls us to plant a church, and that He does the work of spiritual transformation and fruit bearing. How did you juxtapose those two beliefs when the church plant in Chicago failed?

One of the truths that we have learned over the years is that it's not about what you do but who you're becoming in the process. We certainly go after the dreams God puts in our hearts, but ultimately, none of it matters compared to the journey, the maturation process God is taking us through—that we may become more and more like Christ.

After Chicago, were you afraid to start another plant in D. C.? How did you/do you battle fear? I'm thinking specifically of women who are fearful or unsure but whose husbands are gung ho, fearless leaders charging forward. What advice/encouragement would you give them?

I do have a husband who seems fearless sometimes. We've learned that we balance each other out. His "the sky is the limit" dreams and my "down to earth" realism help us balance the risk/reward debate. Everyone should allow God to stretch them. For my husband, being stretched may mean being more patient in going after things. For me, it may mean going after things faster than I'm comfortable with. But understanding that differences are an asset and a blessing is a key to balancing those differences.

National Community Church and Mark's writing and speaking ministry have exploded. How do you maintain a sane marriage and family life with so many demands on your time?

By understanding that you *never* arrive. You never fully achieve balance. As soon as you do, things change again. So if you get into the mindset that it's a constant work in progress, it will work a lot better. You have to always be reevaluating things, re-prioritizing, shifting, changing, and communicating. We have a few boundaries that we have set in place that we try to maintain. On Mark's day off, the two of us always go out for coffee to talk about how things are going. He also determined a set number of days that he would be gone each year—no more. You can put some things in place to help achieve balance. But depending on the season of life, you often have to add or subtract certain things to put the balance back in place.

CHAPTER SEVEN

the Peaceful Heart

BATTLING STRESS

Years ago, at the church Kyle and I attended during seminary, the worship team sang a song about thirst. The chorus repeated one line over and over: "Is anyone thirsty? Anyone?" The first time we sang it, I looked around, almost expecting the ushers to come forward carrying trays of paper cups filled with water. *Yes, as a matter of fact, I am quite thirsty*, I realized. When you sing about it for five minutes straight, a cool cup of water is almost all you can think about.

An Understandable Thirst

During the past few months, I have run myself ragged. I am thirsty for spiritual and emotional rest, a word of encouragement from the Lord, a fresh look at the big picture, and time to reflect and evaluate. Thirsty for God. Thirsty for the mental space to think on and remember what He has done. Thirsty to get off the church planting merry-go-round and just be. Thirsty to lay down all my responsibilities and simply receive from the Lord. A cool cup of spiritual water is almost all I can think about.

Knowing this, my husband sent me away to rest. His urgent plea for me to go, even at the expense of his own physical stamina, confirmed the depth of my stress. Although I only traveled forty-five miles away, I left the demands and routines of daily life and ministry for a blessed two days of reading, reflecting, praying, journaling, sleeping, drinking coffee, and shopping, all of which combined to rejuvenate my soul. When I got in the car to return home, it was with a fresh sense of life and purpose. That thirst for God—the kind that had me looking around for months for a cool cup of water—had been both quenched and joyfully increased.

However, as the city limits disappeared in the rearview mirror and I sped toward home, stress started building, flooding my heart with anxiety and despair at the thought of returning to the routines and demands of life. As I started composing a mental to-do list—invite the new family over for dinner, make a discipleship plan for a midweek meeting with a young woman, prepare for small group, brainstorm ideas for women's ministry—bitter frustration bubbled to the surface. I had spent my days away praying through these very things and offering my burdens to the Lord. He had graciously taken them, speaking peace and joy into my life. But now, after two days of relief, the heavy weight and burden of church planting fell on my heart with a resounding thud. Stress, my familiar foe, had returned.

I wondered if church planting was supposed to be a burden of all work and no joy.

The Stressful Demands of Church Planting

It certainly feels sometimes that this church planting lifestyle is meant to be stressful and burdensome; that it's impossible to start and grow a church while also experiencing peace, rest, and joy; that we are supposed to give every last ounce of ourselves until we have nothing left to give.

Church planting is indeed a stressful endeavor, not just for the church planter but for his wife and family as well. In one study of thirty-four church planting wives, all of the wives reported that they were physically exhausted. Most reported difficulty in keeping a balance between church, home, and work, and 60 percent reported shouldering responsibility for more than one major ministry in the church plant.[13] The study reflects both the physical demands and the spiritual and emotional exhaustion that accompanies church planting work.

Should it be this difficult and demanding?

A healthy amount of stress will definitely be involved because of the hard work and sacrifice required, but must this ministry inevitably lead to burnout, physical exhaustion, health issues, and fractured marriages?

In church planting, it is easy to normalize unhealthy stress and forget that the work doesn't have to be a personally detrimental endeavor. I believe that many church plants fail because of unhealthy stress—most often the undue stress the planter and his wife place on themselves and the expectations they allow others to place on them. Let's look at the most common stressors church planting wives face:

Stressor #1: Confusion about the Role

As the wives of church planters, determining our role in the church plant is especially difficult. In the early stages of the plant, we are called on to lead or help in several ministries, if not all, many of which we are not inclined toward or gifted for. We quickly forget what we *are* gifted for or passionate about and get weighed down with activities that sap our emotional energy. We may also discover that people in our church have varying ideas and expectations of what our role should be.

Stressor #2: Unclear Boundaries

One church planting study found that "ambiguity is endemic to ministry. All members of the [clergy] family participate either directly or indirectly in the church. There is some role expectation of the congregation which must be fulfilled by the minister, his spouse, and even his children. This level of ambiguity causes high levels of stress for clergy spouses."[14] Because of its all-encompassing nature, boundary ambiguity is a hallmark of church planting. In marriage, we talk about ministry. With children in tow, we host ministry events. Our home becomes the hub of the church. In our community, our service and relationships are often synonymous with ministry. Stress multiplies when it seems that nothing is ours—our husbands, homes, time, not even ourselves—or when everything in our lives revolves around ministry.

Stressor #3: Relationships

Relationships are the bedrock of church planting work. The church planter and his wife spend an inordinate amount of time and energy initiating, pursuing, maintaining, and deepening relationships.

At the beginning of church planting, the relationship stress comes from *not* having many of them. Getting to know people and earning their respect requires vast amounts of emotional and physical energy.

In the middle and later stages of church planting, relationship stress comes from efforts to maintain and deepen existing relationships while constantly initiating new ones. Deeper relationships also mean that we are intimately invested in the lives of others through counseling, leading, discipling, and helping. This level of involvement in relationships can be burdensome and exhausting.

Stressor #4: Unfulfilled Expectations

The expectations we have going into a church plant are often unmet. When the expected exponential numerical growth, favor in the community, or life transformations do not come right away—or at all—it can be stressful and overwhelming for the church planter and his family.

Stressor #5: Lack of Support Systems

The stresses of church planting are compounded by a lack—or perceived lack—of physical, emotional, and spiritual support. Some church planting wives, living far from family or familiar surroundings, feel physically isolated. They lack tangible support, such as babysitting or help in the church plant. Family and friends back "home" seem distant and unconcerned.

Feelings of isolation, along with the difficulty of the work, create a vacuum of emotional and spiritual support. In the church plant, the church planter and his wife are the leaders and may not feel that they have anyone to turn to for encouragement or assistance.

The church planting wife in particular may isolate herself because she feels she must be superwoman, not allowing herself to have needs or ask for help. Or she may be eager to share herself with others, but find that her season of life and ministry role leave her feeling isolated because of how little time she has for building connections.

Stressor #6: Marriage

Church planting husbands can either be the wife's stress reliever or her greatest stressor. Stress builds in a marriage when the church planting husband does not understand or at least attempt to understand how the church planting process affects his wife. If he does not make his family a priority, if he fails to appreciate his wife's integral role in the plant, or if he fails to protect her and help her navigate through, a wife may feel unhappy and that the church plant is too heavy of a burden on the family.

At different points in our church planting process, I have battled each of these stressors. That day, driving home from my personal retreat, combating the rising stress, I cried out to God. *Where has the joy gone, Lord? Is church planting supposed to be this way—all work and no joy?* I felt panicky, my mind racing a thousand different directions. I wanted desperately to turn the car around and retreat back to the safe, peaceful confines of the coffee shop I had just left, where life was simple and undemanding. His presence enveloped me as He gently whispered, "*Peace, child.*" My mind stilled as the Spirit directed my thoughts. He reminded me of the truths I have learned and re-learned throughout this process: He is the initiator, and I am the responder. He is the grower, and I am the sower. He is in control, and I am not. Most importantly, He is Peace, not the author of unhealthy stress.

By failing to remember these truths, I was creating my own stress. I recalled how much time I had spent in the months prior to my personal retreat listening to the "shoulds" of ministry and the perceived expectations of others rather than the Lord's whispers of direction. He intended for me to experience peace, even in the busyness of the season. As I released control (or acknowledged that I never had it in the first place) and stepped back into my appropriate place of faithful responder, assurance and peace gripped my heart. I returned home knowing that if I listened for His direction and leadership, He would keep my heart in perfect peace, despite the very real busyness and difficulty of church planting.

In my specific worries about our schedule, I knew that He would care for me by providing opportunities for rest and retreat (that I must take), for connection with my husband, and for time with my family away from ministry. I also recalled the simple priorities He had given me and resolved not to create my own burdens by adding to them. I knew His protection and leadership. In that moment, I experienced what Scripture promises: "You will keep in perfect peace him whose mind is steadfast, because he trusts in you" (Isaiah 26:3 NIV).

Busy but Balanced

In reading Paul's letters in the Bible, we find his accounts of suffering and sacrifice for the sake of the gospel. Labor, toil, and conflict appear as themes in his missionary work. In the face of what we would call "stress," he constantly offered his heavy spiritual burdens to the Lord, followed where the Spirit led him (rather than the "shoulds"), and spoke of joy even as he faced difficult circumstances and constant demands.

Jesus faced an even more overwhelming ministry load, with people constantly demanding His attention. Although He experienced fatigue, He never grew frazzled.

All the gospel writers notice Jesus' busyness, although Mark in particular highlights it. At one point Jesus' family tries to stage an intervention because he is so busy. "Then he went home, and the crowd gathered again, so that they could not even eat. And when his family heard it, they went out to seize him, for they were saying, 'He is out of his mind!'" (Mark 3:20–21). Given the sacredness in the ancient world of eating together, Jesus' life seems out of balance. But he loves people and has the power to help, so he has one interruption after another . . . If we love people and have the power to help, then we are going to be busy. . . . In the midst of outer busyness we can develop an inner quiet.[15]

Developing an inner quiet—a peaceful heart—similar to Jesus' is our goal, and we must move toward it purposefully. A frazzled, disjointed way of life does not have to be our "normal." Worry and anxiety are sins, after all, and Jesus, who we pattern our lives after, is named the

Prince of Peace. If our lives are to reflect the One we follow, we must cultivate an inner quiet in the midst of outer busyness like He did. Jesus' life shows us how.

Jesus spent time with His Father.

Once Jesus began His ministry, He was constantly on the move, healing the sick, preaching to the masses, and teaching His disciples. At one point, He encouraged His men to take a break because, in the busyness of their ministry schedule, they had not even had a chance to eat (Mark 6:31).

Scripture reveals the secret of how He maintained such a grueling schedule, and how He continually gave of Himself: He went off on His own to pray and commune with His Father. At times, with the demanding crowds closing in, He stole small windows of opportunity to be alone with God. Less frequently, but often before pivotal moments—preaching the Sermon on the Mount, calling His disciples to follow, preparing for the cross—He spent entire nights in prayer.

Communion with God is the way to peace. This is a promise.

Why? What was He praying about? Despite His deity, His human body needed spiritual rest and rejuvenation. Perhaps, also, He prayed for His followers, that they would fulfill their calling well and be strengthened for the task ahead. Surely He prayed with compassion for those to whom He preached. More than anything, I imagine, these moments fed His craving for communion with His source of joy and friendship. From His Father, He got both His marching orders and His fuel for ministry.

Jesus' actions model for us what a healthy life of ministry and service look like. He was compassionate and gracious, bold and purposeful, and He was also extremely busy. However, He placed communion with God as the hub, the fuel, the catalyst, and the source of all He did. He prioritized time with God over all other good things: "And when He had sent the multitudes away, He went up on the mountain by Himself to pray. Now when evening came, He was alone there" (Matthew 15:23).

Jesus understood that prayer, when done right, is not a spiritual discipline but an act of utter dependence on the Father. He knew that, like nutrients to a body, receiving from and being with God nurtures the soul. Cares and concerns, the combatants of peace, can only be laid down through prayer. Prayer, in turn, replaces what has been laid down with peace. This is likely why Jesus taught us to pray, "Give us this day our daily bread," because each day, with its cares and worries, requires our dependence, our abiding in the Source.

We often associate peace with changed circumstances or a lack of busyness, but as Jesus modeled, God's peace comes through dependence in the midst of busyness. Approaching God through prayer, Bible reading, and worship, in which we bring our needy selves to receive from Him, are acts of need. Peace comes through this dependence, through ceding control into more capable hands. When we go to Him and let the truth of His capabilities wash over us, He washes away our anxiety. However, if we do not consistently spend time with the Source of peace, we cannot achieve spiritual rest by any other means, not with sleep or food or physical rest. Over a period of time, without spiritual nourishment, we become prime candidates for ministry burnout, in which normal, everyday stress develops into paralyzing exhaustion.

Communion with God is the way to peace. This is a promise. "Be anxious for nothing, but in everything by prayer and supplication, with thanksgiving, let your requests be made known to God; and the peace of God, which surpasses all understanding, will guard your hearts and minds through Christ Jesus" (Philippians 4:6–7).

Jesus had priorities.

If we are to model our ministries after Jesus, we will sacrificially give of our time, talents, and treasures. We will have compassion for the masses that moves us to action. We will obey the Father's will. And like Him, we will be busy. In Scripture, though, Jesus does not attempt to meet the needs of every person He encounters. He is purposeful and strategic.

One of His most fascinating ministry strategies is how He allocated His time. He spent the majority of His three-year ministry with twelve guys, and the largest chunk of that time with just three—Peter, James, and John. With a history-changing message to circulate and a grandiose goal of reaching all people in all generations, His philosophy of spending most of His time with just a few people, frankly, seems strange. But by prioritizing His time and investment, He reproduced Himself in twelve faithful men who, after His death, turned the world upside down (see Acts 17:6).

Our ministry philosophy is often quite the opposite. We try to draw crowds, get involved in as many ministries or volunteer opportunities as possible, and cultivate relationships with everyone we know. The bigger the reach, we think, the greater the impact, so we spread ourselves thin trying to do and be all. However, Jesus modeled that peace comes through simplicity and focus. A well-arranged soul—and a kingdom impact for that matter—comes from a well-arranged life.

God has given us prayer as an act of dependence and a source of strength for ministry. He has also given us limits. In order to live well within our limits, we must maintain clear priorities.

> The Lord always reminds me that *people* are priority over *tasks*.

Priorities, like budgets, usually make us feel guilty; we want to have them, but we don't want to be overly rigid or fail to keep them. We are especially good at helping our husbands maintain their priorities when ministry is encroaching on family time, but may struggle to even define our own. However, priorities provide structure for our lives—what fits within our God-given priorities gets our primary attention and what doesn't fit gets delegated or left undone.

In church planting, defining and maintaining priorities is challenging. With every season and size in the evolution of the church plant, our lives and our ministry opportunities look radically different. Every few months, the Lord nudges me back on course, reminding me to continue refining and narrowing my purpose and priorities.

Some, though, never change, no matter how many times I prayerfully evaluate my life. These are the things that if I neglect, no one can do for me—spending time in the Word, being a wife to Kyle, and loving and training my children. But it gets a little murky after that. What is my specific ministry as a pastor's wife in the church? What relationships in the community should I nurture? Who are the women God wants me to invest in through discipleship?

Priorities can only accomplish what they're meant to when we know who God intended us to be, and we rest in—even celebrate—His plans for us. If He primarily spent His time with only a few, surely there must be freedom and peace in becoming women of few and fixed passions. If He did not heal and touch everyone He met yet ended His ministry with a statement of completeness ("It is finished"), He does not intend for us to do and be everything to everyone. He knows we are finite people. He made us that way, after all.

Each time I discuss my priorities with the Lord, He reminds me that *people* are priority over *tasks.* In our lives, certain people are priorities above any others: our husbands and children. The time we spend with them yields the most important fruit. Our family relationships must receive the majority of our service, attention, love, and energy. We must be careful that ministry does not always encroach on these relationships, where our time with the Lord becomes about ministry, our conversations with our husbands focus on ministry, or our children are shuffled around town because of ministry. We must maintain our priorities, and we must also protect those priorities from being dominated by ministry.

Jesus rested.

"Then the apostles gathered to Jesus and told Him all things, both what they had done and what they had taught. And He said to them, 'Come aside by yourselves to a deserted place and rest a while.' For there were many coming and going, and they did not even have time to eat. So they departed to a deserted place in the boat by themselves" (Mark 6:30–32).

> As church planting wives, we are doers. We struggle with resting well.

The multitudes pulled at Jesus and His disciples to meet their spiritual and physical needs. There was much to do, always. As Jesus and the disciples gathered together, debriefing all that had happened, Jesus did not send them out again until after they rested. He knew something that they didn't yet—that an integral aspect of ministry is silence, rest, and reflection.

We live in a loud world. Our lives are overloaded with activities, appointments, to-do lists, and meetings. It's exhausting, this constant commotion. Despite the exhaustion, silence and stillness often make me uncomfortable.

The lies, too, come in the silence and stillness . . . lies that tell me activity is spiritual, movement is communion, that tasks bring life.

You are not doing enough.

You are alone. Everyone else is together.

This is a waste of precious time.

People who matter are busy doing important things.

My flesh runs from silence and stillness, yet it's most what I need. When I sit in silence with my discomfort, letting my heart and mind settle, and after I wade through and wrestle the lies into submission, I find life that no amount of interaction, activity, or mind-numbing entertainment can bring.

God is always in the silence, in my rest, waiting there to be heard and enjoyed, if I will just listen.

> Whoever will listen will hear the speaking Heaven. This is definitely not the hour when men take kindly to an exhortation to listen, for listening is not today a part of popular religion. We are at the opposite end of the pole from there. Religion has accepted the monstrous heresy that noise, size, activity, and bluster make a man dear to God. But we may take heart. To a people caught in the tempest of the last great conflict God says, "Be still and know that I am God," and still He says it, as if He means to tell us that our strength and safety lie not in noise but in silence.[16]

We are wise women if we listen when God says to us, "Come aside by yourself to a deserted place and rest for a while." We are wiser still when we plan and prepare for times of regular rest through Sabbaths, time away with our husbands, personal retreats, or vacations.

As church planting wives, we are doers. We struggle with resting well. We feel guilty when we say no or when we actually carve out time to rest. Then when we are resting, we feel guilty because we feel like we should be doing something productive. However, when we fail to rest, we disobey God, refuse His safeguard for our hearts, and experience stress rather than peace.

God has given us rest not only as a gift but as a way of acknowledging that we *need*. Like priorities, rest is an act of dependence and trust: *Lord, I am not responsible for everything and everyone, but You are. In my rest, I trust that You are still working.* While we rest, God, who needs nothing, remains at work on our behalf and on behalf of our families and churches.

As we rest, as we give Him our stressors, as we rely on Him for daily strength, He replaces our anxiety with peace. We give Him the guilt-infused "shoulds" that urge us out of balance, and He gives us joy through our simple obedience.

When we follow Jesus' example—when we spend time with the Father, when we maintain His priorities for us, and when we rest—the main stressors still impact our lives, but their ability to frazzle us or feed our fear diminishes. We actually slow down long enough to listen and know when He's calling us to rest or retreat. We can sit in the tension of not fully knowing our role in the church plant because we trust He will show us as we meet with Him. We also have opportunity to cast our cares upon Him rather than running at full speed with heavy burdens on our backs. Our obedience to Jesus' leadership plan grants us peace, for He blesses His own design, and His design is our stress relief.

The Right Pace

Ministry, especially if we intend to *remain* in it for the long haul, demands the pace of a long-distance marathon rather than a sprint. Running for long distances in a healthy way requires taking in nutrients and oxygen as it is also expended. Similarly, in ministry, our health depends on our taking in rest and the food of the Word as we give out to others. We cannot breathe out grace unless we breathe it in ourselves.

I find, too, that my long-distance pace must include healthy boundaries. Sometimes I say yes and sometimes I say no. Sometimes I take on responsibility and sometimes I don't. Sometimes I spend time with people and sometimes I don't. I breathe in, I breathe out.

At least I'm learning to. The longer I run this marathon, the more

I realize how fluid boundaries are. Boundaries cannot be placed on a checklist, as much as I would like to sometimes. They are not often as simple as a yes or a no. Boundaries require our utter dependence on the Lord's direction. In various seasons of life, He has us doing and relating in vastly different ways.

For this moment, in this mile, wherever we are, we breathe in His direction and breathe out obedience.

The problem, obviously, comes when others have different ideas about our pace. In His ministry, Jesus encountered this same issue, as recorded in John 6:15: "Therefore when Jesus perceived that they (the crowds) were about to come and take Him by force to make Him king, He departed again to the mountain by Himself alone."

The race spectators, many God-seeking people, wanted Jesus to take the kingly authority, power, and glory He deserved. Not a bad thing. But it wasn't what God intended for Him, and Jesus knew it. So He withdrew from the crowds, perhaps to erect a boundary, to make a gentle statement: *This is not what God has asked Me to do. I want to be obedient to Him alone.*

> We do well to follow Jesus' example, to let God set our pace instead of the crowds.

In that moment, in that mile, He breathed in His Father's direction and breathed out graceful obedience.

I doubt the crowds understood or liked it. They might have grumbled against Him. But if He had listened, giving in to their ideas and allowing them to influence His pace, we would not have His ministry to us on the cross.

We do well to follow Jesus' example, to let God set our pace instead of the crowds. The crowds have their own ideas, sometimes very good ones, but with limited perspective. If we follow God's lead, no matter if others misunderstand, He will lead us in a way that enables our fruitful race all the way to the finish line.

Today, in this moment, in this mile of the race, simply breathe in His direction and breathe out obedience.

This is how we pace ourselves.

This is how we develop a peaceful heart.

Cultivating Your Heart

Do you identify with the sources of stress identified in this chapter (confusion about the role, unclear boundaries, relationships, unfulfilled expectations, lack of a support system, marriage)? Are there ways in which you might be creating your own stress or adding to already stressful situations?

How can you apply Jesus' example to each area?

- Are you making prayer, Bible reading, meditation a true priority in your daily routine?
- Can you make changes in the way you pace yourself?
- Do you need to remove those "guilt-infused *shoulds*"?
- Do you need to revisit your priorities in home life, ministry, and other responsibilities or obligations?
- Discuss your needs with your husband and determine practical ways you can get rest and relief, e.g., an evening out, two hours alone.

Scriptures to encourage you: Psalms 23; 27; 16:8; 55:22; 121:7–8; Philippians 4:6; John 14:27; Isaiah 40:30–31; Malachi 4:2; Romans 12:2; Habakkuk 3:17–19; Matthew 11:28–30; Philippians 4:13; 1 Thessalonians 5:16–18.

Interview with

Curtis and Amanda Jones launched Bayou City Fellowship in Houston on September 11, 2011. They have two children.

What did you learn about yourself and the Lord in the first year of planting?

I've learned more and more that God is trustworthy and faithful. I kept a journal during 2011 to record the ways God answered our prayers and showed us His power. It was impossible to keep track of all the things He did—there were so many! We were way out on a limb with God, but the view of His faithfulness was spectacular.

What I've learned about myself is that I'm absolutely desperate for God's grace! Still! I don't have what it takes to be a pastor's wife. And I certainly don't deserve to be one. The first time I read your blog, I wondered why you had titled it *Grace Covers Me* because it didn't scream "church planting" to me. About five minutes into our launch, I understood. I'm desperate for His grace every single second of the day.

You are planting in your hometown, perhaps even trying to reach people you've known for a long time. Your surroundings haven't changed, but how has your perspective changed regarding your city? What are the joys and difficulties of planting in your hometown?

I feel less like the city is here for the good of my family and more like my family is here for the good of the city. I'm very aware that everything I do outside of my home is an opportunity to share the gospel in word and in deed. (And really, that goes for inside the home, too.)

We have definitely seen advantages and disadvantages to planting in our hometown. On one hand, we know the city well and have a lot of support here. My family is very close, and their support has been wonderful. It's so much fun when my mom and I are scheduled to work with the children on the same day. I love seeing the passion she has for the Word expressed in that context. And Curtis always has an encouraging message from her waiting on his phone whenever we leave church.

Curtis and I spent a few months serving in England and then the next three years serving in Irving, Texas, so I do not take it for granted that we're getting to do this in my hometown.

On the other hand, since we already have a lot of relationships in place here in Houston, we have to get over ourselves and not be offended or take it personally if everyone—even a friend—we invite to church doesn't jump on board. And if they do come, we can't be bitter if they don't decide to join us. That would be miserable.

I think the hardest part of this journey was when we were sharing our vision for BCF with friends in an effort to put together our core team. Waiting to see who God was calling to join us or not was difficult. It was a very raw, vulnerable, and emotionally charged time. I'm glad to be done with that season and thankful that Jesus got us through it! Ultimately, the Lord crafted an incredible core team that has blown us away with their faith and hard work. He knew exactly what He was doing when He called each one.

In our first year, we experienced a lot of spiritual warfare. Has that been the case for you and Curtis? How have you recognized it and how have you responded?

Oh my, yes. Nothing could have prepared us for the spiritual warfare we have experienced. My husband has very little fear, almost to a fault. But at this time last year, he was afraid to fall asleep at night because he had an overwhelming dread of waking up blind and deaf. And his dreams always had a snake in them. For months the enemy also attacked me with very destructive dreams. His tactics weren't hard to recognize, but they were hard to endure. We finally started speaking up about it and a lot of people prayed for us. Right after our launch, some couples on our core team took shifts praying for us throughout the night so that we could get some rest. We didn't know about it until the next morning, but their prayers worked. For now, God has brought that particularly intense battle to an end.

There is a ton of pressure associated with church planting. How do you help ease the pressure Curtis might feel? How does he help ease any pressure you might feel?

I remember one particularly crushing day last spring when the pressure was extremely intense. I told Curtis I didn't want to talk to anybody outside of our family, and I sent him out to rent a movie while I ordered enough pizza to feed a small army. Pizza and a movie aren't necessarily bad, but in that case we were bypassing Jesus and taking our broken, stressed-out hearts straight to food and entertainment. Not good!

I think the best way we've learned to ease the pressure for each other is to pray together. We aren't always good about keeping up that habit when we don't feel stressed, and that's something we need to work on.

CHAPTER EIGHT

the Undivided Heart

CHOOSING TO PLEASE GOD ALONE

I have conversations with people in my head all the time. I didn't recognize that I did this until recently, when I traced my anxiety and frustration back to my morning shower. An innocent, almost passing thought had turned into an internal knockdown, drag-out fight in between shampoo, rinse, and conditioner.

A Silent Conversation

Someone popped into my mind.

Then something positive they said about someone else came to mind.

Then I compared myself and my choices to that someone else. I am quite different than that someone else.

So in my illogical thinking, that someone likes that someone else and does not like me. (Got that?)

Thus began the conversation in my head, in which I stated the case for why that someone *and* that someone else should like and respect and approve of me.

Then, strangely, I put words in that someone's mouth in response to my own. Negative words. Accusing words. Debating words. Cutting words.

Before I realized it, I had spent the better part of an hour having made-up conversations with several people, all of them negative, depressing, and frustrating.

Suddenly, I awoke to the truth of what was happening.

Those people weren't really saying those things to me, but I knew who was. The Liar. The Thief. The Accuser. He had taken everything I already accuse myself of and planted it in the mouths of people I love.

And I had believed him. I had allowed him to steal, kill, and destroy. If I hadn't awoken to truth, I might have even let him bring subtle division and isolation between me and that someone and that someone else.

Then I thought about all the times I have let him do that to me, how I give him and his lies an audience:

People don't like you, but quite possibly you can persuade them to. Make all your decisions based on this idea.

You are chained to this way of thinking and believing and acting. You cannot change; it's hopeless.

Hide yourself from others, so they don't see how you are lacking.

What you're doing doesn't really matter.

What Did I Do Wrong?

In the enemy's scenarios, I am always disliked, disrespected, lacking, or doing the wrong things. His lies divide my heart right in two, one half sincerely desiring to please God, the other half desperately concerned with what people think of me and actively strategizing how to win their approval. Unfortunately, his scenarios usually involve aspects of ministry, our church, or relationships in our church. There is something about church planting that exacerbates my struggles with people pleasing. It is a battle I fight every day as I make decisions, allocate my time, and direct my thoughts and emotions.

Take, for instance, an interaction I had with a fellow mom, a neighborhood acquaintance. In striking up conversation, we discovered we had many things in common: our soccer-playing children attended the same preschool, our oldest sons attended the same elementary school and already knew each other, and we each were both stay-at-home moms. When she asked me where my husband worked, I told her about our church and invited her and her family to visit.

Over the course of church planting, I have had many similar conversations and can usually discern whether they will accept my invitation. With her, I felt confident that I'd see her again and thanked God for the possibility of this strong, stable family joining our community of faith.

Sure enough, she sent her husband to our church on a scouting trip a few weeks later. I spotted him soon after he entered, chatted with him, introduced him to my husband, and invited him to sit with our family. He was engaged in the service and left with a promise to return with his family. Kyle, following up with him during the week, thanked him for coming and invited him to return with his whole family, to which he responded positively.

> Perhaps she didn't like me as much as I had liked her.

But the following Sunday, they didn't come.

Again, the next Sunday, they didn't show.

For a few more weeks, I anticipated their visit, but they never came back.

Of course, this is not the first person to visit and not return, but this time I was unusually disappointed. The husband had visited our church at my invitation; had he also not returned because of me? After all, I was the one who had greeted him and answered his questions about the church. Had I said something wrong? Mostly I was disappointed because I had connected easily with the wife. Perhaps she didn't like me as much as I had liked her.

I have done this dozens of times. Someone leaves the church, and I wonder what I could have done differently to keep them from leaving. A small problem is mentioned, and I'm gripped by an urgency to fix it so that that person will be happy. I teach a Bible study or counsel a college girl and then leave analyzing what I said. An invitation comes and I feel that I have to go to the event, even if it is at the expense of my family, because I don't want to hurt the hostess's feelings. I urge my husband to smooth over a conflict because I am not comfortable until it is settled. I want to appease everyone. I make decisions based upon the expectations of others.

I want to be liked.

In the case of the family not returning, I couldn't rest easy knowing that they might not have liked our church. I racked my brain, trying to uncover what they had not liked, ready to scrap everything and start over just for the sake of this family's approval and attendance.

Clearly, what I was really wondering is why they didn't like *me*.

All these thoughts, anxieties, and questions that take up an inordinate amount of mental space serve to illustrate my divided heart. I want to please God, but I also want to please people. If pleasing God means the displeasure, misunderstanding, or criticism of people, I am pulled between two masters.

People Pleasing

I doubt I am alone in my penchant toward people pleasing. It seems to be an innate, fleshly struggle for women. However, church planting wives, who are out in front leading and serving, face the temptation almost daily.

In order to be effective disciples, helpmates, mothers, and ministry helpers, we must keep our hearts undivided, where we are both fueled and driven by the pleasure of God rather than the pleasure of people.

If we allow ourselves to become people focused in church planting, we become dependent on others for encouragement and affirmation (and what they give is never enough). We make decisions that put us in the best light possible. When presented with a ministry opportunity, we mentally scroll through the names and faces of people who will be disappointed if we don't do it. We avoid difficult situations or conversations because we don't want people to see us fail. We fear doing what God wants us to do because of what others will say or think. We constantly feel the weight of other people's expectations. Our ministry becomes diluted and impotent because it is fueled by self, not the Spirit. We are never satisfied or at rest, and when criticism comes, we buckle. We are unable to celebrate how God uses others. We become self-absorbed behind the guise of ministry. Unable to follow God's leadership for fear of upsetting someone, we miss our true calling in our family or ministry. Most dire of all, Paul says that if we are people pleasers, we are not actually serving Christ: "Am I now seeking human approval, or God's approval? Or am I trying to please people? If I were still pleasing people, I would not be a servant of Christ" (Galatians 1:10 NRSV).

People pleasing is a secret sin that tortures us. It is a cancer that drains the power behind our ministry, paralyzes us, and eats away at our hearts. In order to be faithful, our daily war against people pleasing is a necessary fight, which starts with recognizing the vast discrepancy between the approval of people and the approval of God. We must recognize that fully depending on other people— our husbands, friends, family members, church members—cannot and will not sustain us. The *only* thing that will enable us to be effective and joyful church planting wives on a long-term basis is being with Him, hearing and receiving from Him, and following His leadership.

> God nudged me. He said, *My love for you is immense, immeasurable.*

One summer on a trip to the beach with our family, I found myself unable to settle in and enjoy the vacation. Sitting on the balcony overlooking the beach, praying through the unrest in my heart one morning, I saw Kyle and our boys playing along the shoreline. From my perch, they looked so little compared to the ocean. I realized I had spent most of the week walking along the beach looking down, helping the kids look for seashells or chasing crabs. When I took time to actually look at the ocean reaching from horizon to horizon in all directions, God nudged me. *What you see in front of you is so vast, so deep, so powerful with waves, and yet it is just a tiny sliver of the entire ocean. That is like My love for you. It is immense, immeasurable. Now look at your husband and your children playing on the beach. They have no power to tame the ocean, like I do. Pursuing their approval or anyone else's is like looking for a small love while ignoring the powerful, all-encompassing love around you. When you are filled up by My love, you will not need or seek the approval of others.*

Is it any wonder that we are fascinated by the ocean, drawn to it for relaxation and to escape the busyness of our days? The ocean is a picture of God's love and grace continually pounding over us. Its powerful waves, just like God's love, grind the hardest stones to sand. Each crest pounding onto the shore speaks love, constant and forever, a love that cannot be compared to any human love.

His love is big, dwarfing any acceptance or approval we can draw from others. Knowing this love is the first step in fighting and winning our battle with people pleasing because:

"If God is for us, who can be against us? He who did not spare His own Son, but delivered Him up for us all, how shall He not with Him also freely give us all things?" (Romans 8:31–32).

We must know that God, our great Father, is for us. A good father loves by protecting his children and providing for them. A *great* father goes beyond protecting and providing, however. A great father expresses his approval of his children and extends his blessing to them. With his approval, he says, "I like you. I am for you." His extended blessing acts as an emotional inheritance: "I will give you everything I have. I am investing myself in you. I am joyfully passing on my name and my heritage to you."

God is not just a good Father. He is a *great* Father. He gives Himself willingly and completely to His spiritual children. We see it with David and Solomon. God's blessings and mercy continue toward them even after their deaths, for Jesus came through their lineage. In fact, His blessing and approval toward them even extend to us today through the One who came from them. It is a lineage of approval and blessing.

If we are in Christ, our Father extends that same approval toward us. He has even given us a seal of approval so that we might not doubt it: "God . . . has given us the Spirit as a guarantee" (2 Corinthians 5:5).

The Holy Spirit's presence in our hearts assures us that we are no longer slaves but sons and daughters; no longer outcasts but chosen. We are included in the inheritance of Jesus. We enjoy the same blessing that God bestowed on David and Solomon.

Unlike a withholding earthly father, we don't have to clamor for God's approval or attention. We can rest in the strong arms of our Father, assured that we have His attention, blessing, and approval. We have His heart. He is for us. His approval will never, ever go away. When we know this, really know this, we don't need to look anywhere else for approval.

Choosing the God-Thermometer

Sometimes we *should* consider the opinions and thoughts of others. When we are a part of authentic community, our lives should be informed by those who know us and seek our good. For example, if a faithful friend prayerfully and lovingly highlights one of my blind spots, I shouldn't discount her insight. But I cannot measure my *value* or my *success* in ministry according to the opinions or expectations of others. We must measure success and define ourselves according to God's vocabulary.

In life and in church planting, faith is the victory. God is not evaluating our good works but rather is looking for our faithfulness. Faithfulness means obedience—when God leads, we act. Faithfulness also means perseverance—we are consistently obedient. Our faithful obedience to the Lord pleases Him and also commends us before others. It speaks for us. And if people misunderstand or criticize, we can return to the Lord to determine if we are successful, if we have truly been faithful to His leading. God may not allow us to see how He is using us in our churches or our cities, but the God-focused church planting wife knows that results and the affirmation of others don't measure her success. Faithfulness does.

If we rely on the wrong thermometer, we fall into despair or cater to others, trying to alter the reading.

My car is outfitted with a digital thermometer. In the winter, on the way to school each morning, my boys and I check the outside temperature from the warmth of our car. After pulling out from the garage, the numbers tick ever lower and my middle son gleefully screams out each lowered degree. On unusually cold mornings, we estimate how low the numbers will drop, hoping to beat our previous record low.

Every day, whether I do so consciously or not, I take my own temperature, too. Not my physical temperature but the one that measures my success as a wife, mom, or helper in ministry. And every day, you take your own temperature, measuring what you are doing well and what others think of you. Sometimes—to our detriment—we take our temperature with a people-thermometer: Do they think I'm doing a good job as a church planting wife? Do they like me? Do they see and appreciate what I'm doing? What do they expect from me? How can I meet their expectations?

Our goal and our need is to take our temperature solely with a God-thermometer: Am I serving Him joyfully and obediently? Is He pleased? What does He want me to do? What is He saying to me? Am I being faithful to Him?

Sometimes the temperature reads the same on both thermometers— God affirms our faithful obedience to His leadership and then someone else also affirms how He has used us in their lives. However, tension develops when the thermometers read differently. For example, if we have obeyed God's leading but someone misunderstands, reading the people-thermometer gives a false reading. If we rely on the wrong thermometer, we fall into despair or cater to others, trying to alter the reading. But taking our temperature using the God-thermometer gives us the assurance and peace that come from obedience. Happily, if we read His thermometer only, we always get a *correct* reading—He either affirms our faithfulness or gently corrects us.

What about you? Which thermometer are you using to measure your value and to guide your decisions? You can know that you're using a God-thermometer if you:

- Evaluate what you will be involved in through prayer and conversations with your husband. You do not respond to urgent pleas or according to what you know people want from you.
- Wait for God's leadership, trusting that the Lord will give you direction on all matters.
- Aspire to serve without seeking or expecting acknowledgment. You appreciate receiving these blessings, but they do not motivate your service. You enjoy serving in unseen ways.

- Act in obedience to the Lord, even if it means uncertainty, difficulty, discomfort, or possibly being misunderstood.
- Are primarily concerned with submission and obedience before God. The majority of your thoughts are on Him, not on what others think of you.
- Feel comfortable being yourself and using the gifts God gave you.
- Freely worship and receive from the Lord at church instead of focusing on how others are evaluating you.
- Don't leave conversations or interactions analyzing everything you said or did, questioning whether you are liked. Your heart is at rest.
- Are bold, not held back by insecurity or fear.

Is it possible to become women unaffected by the opinions of others? Though it is a daily battle, I believe that the more we use our God-thermometers, the more His love and approval will become all we need, and the more we will rest in God's calling on our lives.

Assured of God's Approval

In Christ, God's approval is constant, but, unfortunately, our grasp of it is not. We cannot grasp it fully in one sitting, like a child gulping down a large cup of water. In our human limits, we are only able to receive it in small, regular intervals. We *need* it in small, regular intervals. After a drink of God's grace, we run off to play, and our thirst causes us to forget our previous satiation.

A thirsty child doesn't question her thirst. She immediately asks for a drink. Similarly, we must regularly return to our Source of satiation for reassurance, for a reminder of God's approval.

In order to conquer people pleasing, we must daily depend on the Spirit as our Source of power and daily set Christ as our focus. We must make it a practice to take concerns, cares, thoughts, and struggles to Him, including the expectations we perceive others have of us so that we might prayerfully evaluate if we are making ministry decisions based upon pleasing people or pleasing God.

Sometimes we know God's approval, but we need to go to Him for reassurance that we're on the right track, that He's bearing fruit in and through us.

Jesus reminded His disciples several times that He came to serve, not to be served. If we have the same mind as Christ, we will be willing to give of ourselves, even when we don't receive encouragement or affirmation in return. In church planting, this may be especially difficult because we may give for *years* without seeing much return for our work. We may constantly feel invisible and unappreciated. We are able to serve and give like Christ only when our source, motivation, and approval come from Him.

The Comparison Game

People pleasing has a close cousin: comparison. When we are concerned about the opinions of others, we have a tendency to compare ourselves with others: other church planting wives, other mothers, other churches, and on and on. We are, once again, seeking to meet a man-made or self-made standard, or win the respect of others. This tendency is especially difficult when we are discouraged in church planting or our church is struggling.

Both people pleasing and comparison feed on our insecurities and our pride, but neither is right and neither is based on a correct understanding of God's character.

Comparison has been one of my greatest struggles in church planting.

I think about this when I go to the bank to make a deposit. The bank teller always gives my children the exact same colored lollipops. I have never asked him to do this, but, without fail, he digs through the lollipop basket until he finds a matching set of Dum Dums.

He must be a dad because he knows about the fight he is saving me. The one where all of my boys are eyeing the lollipops they don't have rather than enjoying the one they do. The one where they fight and whine for their favorite color. The one in which they are not satisfied until they have what their sibling has.

As I drive away from the bank window, I inwardly thank this man and think about this picture of human jealousy: envious, controlling, domineering, possessive, and self-focused.

It is hard not wanting the bright pink lollipop when you have been given the brown one.

The church planting wife will be tempted to compare herself, her gifts, her husband, and her church to others, and these temptations threaten to destroy her joy.

I know, because comparison has been one of my greatest struggles in church planting. Before we even moved to our city, I discovered that another couple was also planning to start a church here at the same time. As I searched their website, little seeds of comparison were planted in my heart.

Less than a week after our move, I met a woman whose husband was a church planter. They were two years ahead of us in the process, so I peppered her with questions about her experience and about their church. I was genuinely interested, but I also allowed those little seeds of comparison to sprout.

After a year of toil and labor but little fruit, another young, eager church planting pastor came to our city looking for a strategic location to start a church. When he chose a location that my husband had been pursuing, the sprouts of comparison in my heart grew into big, green plants. For too many months, I struggled with what happened, constantly comparing our church with theirs and wanting success for us and failure for them. The Lord spoke to me over and over about it, how the comparison was poisoning me and how wicked my thoughts were. Did I really want a church—a group of people intent on sharing the love of Christ—to suffer? I wanted God to love us more, to give us the yummy pink lollipop, while they got the yucky brown one.

The Jealousy Trap

Comparison leads to jealousy and covetousness. It's exactly what happened to Saul as David enjoyed success in battle:

Whatever Saul sent him to do, David did it so successfully that Saul gave him a high rank in the army. This pleased all the people, and Saul's officers as well. When the men were returning home after David had killed the Philistine, the women came out from all the towns of Israel to meet King Saul with singing and dancing, with joyful songs and with tambourines and lutes. As they danced, they sang: "Saul has slain his thousands, and David his tens of thousands." Saul was very angry; this refrain galled him. "They have credited David with tens of thousands," he thought, "but me with only thousands. What more can he get but the kingdom?" And from that time on Saul kept a jealous eye on David. (1 Samuel 18:5–9 NIV)

Was Saul successful as a king and as a warrior? Certainly. But it wasn't enough for him. As he compared himself to David, his pride and insecurities fueled the raging fire of his jealousy. His jealousy spiritually blinded him and eventually destroyed him.

Selfish ambition and discontentment lie at the heart of jealousy. We want to be loved, liked, and respected above all others, so we might have a hard time rejoicing when others are noticed or given recognition. Where jealousy lives, there is not room for two.

Jealousy also distorts our understanding of God. We begin to believe that God should not use or gift anyone else except for us. We will use our "spiritualness" and our God to gain favor in the eyes of men.

The Bible says jealousy is of the flesh and that God opposes the jealous because it questions the wisdom with which He distributes gifts. The result? "A heart at peace gives life to the body, but envy rots the bones" (Proverbs 14:30 NIV). Ultimately, like Saul, unchecked jealousy destroys a true picture of God and obliterates our hearts and our ministries.

> We must also celebrate how God is using others, but not try to imitate them.

God is not like my bank teller. He gives to everyone, but He does not give equally or similarly. He gives perfectly, however, and until we trust that, we will be dissatisfied with what we have been given. As a Father, God knows His kids' tendency to want what their siblings have. But unlike our spiteful jealousy, God's jealousy says, "I absolutely know what is best for you and I want you to have it. Because I love you, I will not let you settle for anything less." He lifts our eyes up to Him and away from watching others and reminds us that He has perfectly and strategically given us our gifts, talents, and ministries.

Therefore, we must know our gifts and use them. We often are too busy watching others to identify how God wants to specifically use us. Instead of faithfully serving, we cower in fear because we are not gifted like the object of our comparison. However, God has designed us to be artists, creating worship using different mediums, tools, and inspirations. God values the art that each of His kids create, the seemingly insignificant, often unseen acts of service just as much as He values those using more "seen" gifts. After all, His definition of success is faithful obedience.

Don't despise your gifts; God certainly doesn't. In fact, it's how He's appointed to receive your worship. As you identify your strengths, ask God to use you, take joy in worshiping God through your gifts, and then thank Him when He does. We must also celebrate how God is using others, but not try to imitate them. When God chooses to use others, rejoice in their success through prayer. Thank God for what He's doing through them and ask for them to receive even greater blessings. Ask God to reaffirm how He wants to use you. If you try to imitate those you wish you were, He doesn't get *your* worship. You are the only one who can be you and I am the only one who can be me. Let's get on with being ourselves!

He wants to use our specific personalities and gifts where He has placed us, but when we are distracted about what He's given other church planting wives or by what others think of us, He cannot use us as He wants. When we are inauthentic followers, God cannot and will not use us to influence others. He wants our hearts. He wants our attention. He wants us to listen for His expectations and His approval, not the weak applause of fellow human beings.

That day, when I had the conversation inside my head, I realized that underneath the lies I believe about others is another layer of lies regarding God, the lies from which stem all other lies and all of my sin:

God has forgotten you.

God withholds His approval from you.

God has let you down.

God loves others more than He loves you.

Liar. Accuser. Thief. Destroyer.

I will not listen to you.

When I awoke both to the lies and to the truth, I ran to God. *Show me truth, God, and help me believe You. Help me pull out the recording playing on repeat in my head and put in one of truth, of reality. I so often listen to the Liar and assume You think the same of me.*

Reality comes in a whisper:

Come to Me and rest, child.

I love you.

You are enough because of the cross. Cling to it.

I am always working on your behalf. I do not sleep or grow weary.

I take delight in you.

Now come, lay down your defenses and fear. Let Me bind your divided heart.

Let Me be enough for you.

Cultivating Your Heart

People pleasing, comparison, and jealousy are all very natural tendencies, yet are unhealthy and unhelpful in church planting (and in every area of life).

Consider 2 Corinthians 5:9. Is it your goal to please Him or someone else? Give this some careful thought.

Evaluate your response in light of the statements on pages 150–51 regarding the God-thermometer that you can use to measure your value and guide your decisions.

Interview with

Jennifer
Carter

*Jennifer Carter is married to Matt, the pastor of the Austin Stone Community
Church in Austin, Texas. They planted the church in 2002
and since then have seen countless lives in Austin transformed.
Jennifer and Matt have three children.*

Define success for a church planting wife.

Success for me occurs when these three roles are priority: first, as
a child of God; second, as a wife to Matt; third, as a mom. I love
ministry, and I adore people, but if I am not careful to guard these three areas
of my life, everything goes downhill quickly!

Regarding being a child of God, are my eyes fixed on Jesus? Is He
my first priority? Am I spending time daily with Him in prayer and in His Word,
repenting of sin and clinging to Him? Am I abiding in Him? Am I listening for the
Spirit's leading in my life on a daily basis? Everything hinges on my relationship
with Jesus! Everything else must be an overflow from this one relationship.

Is my husband my second priority? Am I loving him well, not just
agape (sacrificial) love but *phileo* (affectionate, tender, playful) love as well?
(Titus 2:4). Am I fulfilling my role as helpmate to him? Am I submitting to him
and respecting him and his authority as he submits himself to Jesus? Am I
seeking ways to bless him and his ministry, not harm him? Am I making sure
we are connecting emotionally, spiritually, and physically on a regular and
frequent basis? Am I recognizing the importance and example of the gospel
that our marriage represents to our children and church family?

Are my children my third priority? Am I making sure we have ample
family time each week, including having a family night at least two or three
times a week where we are eating dinner together, communicating about our
lives, playing together, and laughing together? Am I discipling them, teaching
them about God's love for them, and teaching and displaying the gospel to
them by showing them what it looks like for me to repent, confess, and cry out
for Jesus to change me? It would be a great tragedy if, after we pass away, all
of our children walked away from the Lord because we never took the time

to teach them what God is teaching us, or never held up the Ebenezer of the miracles we've seen God accomplish in our midst, and point them to His glory and truth and amazing work in our lives.

How do you deal with the stresses and demands of church planting/church work?

I have learned the hard way how to say no. I have come to accept my human limitations that God has given me. As much as I want to be all things to all people and help everyone I can, have dinner and coffee with everyone who asks, counsel every hurting woman who I meet, I just can't. This was definitely a difficult adjustment for me, but I realized that saying yes to all these other people meant I was saying no to Matt or my kids . . . or Jesus!

But learning no has also been very freeing for me, because now I know that my no to someone means a yes to my family and a yes to Jesus and what He is calling me to do. I can pray and listen as the Spirit leads me to the people He has placed in my life, rather than driving past them to the next event or whatever I had reluctantly said yes to because I knew that's what the person wanted me to say.

This has been especially helpful as the church has grown in ways we never could have imagined. The toll it has taken on Matt and our marriage at times has been extremely hard, but I must say that God has used the hard times in amazing ways and refined us and our marriage for His glory. As the demands and stresses of the church have grown, my three roles that I mentioned above have become increasingly more important. I do what I can when I can to serve the church body, but I am the only person who can support Matt in the ways that he needs me to as his wife. In many ways, that is the most important role that I can fulfill for the church. Many willing and able people can hold babies and serve in all the ways that are needed in the church, but I am the only one who can serve in the role as Matt's wife.

How do you battle against people pleasing?

This is a tough one! Because, first of all, I truly love people and I love spending time with people. But clearly, we don't have the capacity to meet everyone's needs, and if I tried, then the people who need me most would be getting me the least. So learning that saying no to one person, means saying yes to my family has really helped my perspective. Also, knowing and trusting in God to be God for these people has helped as well. He is sovereign and able to do more than I can imagine, so I am able to rest in that. I try to do a lot more praying for people than trying to please them; that seems to work better!

What habits have you incorporated into your life that help you foster a love for God and for the ministry that He's called you to?

Time with Him! He is so faithful, and His Word is so rich. The more I read His Word and spend time with Him, the more deeply I fall in love with Him.

Ideally, I would spend every morning with Him, but this doesn't always happen. I also try to spend an extended amount of time reading the Bible and praying once a week. Every summer, Matt and I plan a trip to get away for a week, just the two of us. This is great for our marriage, but we also spend a huge chunk of time every morning in the Word separately, which is refreshing to our souls after the year of running hard in ministry.

I also love music. I listen to praise and worship music often, which helps me to keep my eyes on the unseen and eternal. I have a heaven playlist that is so good for my soul. It reminds me to set my mind on the things above, not the things that are on earth (Colossians 3:2).

Another habit that has been critical in fostering my love for God and this ministry He's called me to is meeting regularly with women who hold me accountable and point me to Jesus. We have several couples in our life we are truly living life with. We confess our sins to each other and pray for each other. We also have the joy of praying for and serving our church, our city, and the world together with these couples. I am so thankful for these women in my life and their husbands in Matt's life. They truly are helping us to endure in this race!

CHAPTER NINE

the Healed Heart

WHEN CHURCH PLANTING BRINGS WOUNDS

ear Kyle & Christine,

I don't like you.

I read the anonymous letter through once, showed it to my husband, tried unsuccessfully to figure out who sent it, and then tore it into tiny pieces and threw it away. Otherwise, I would have memorized and stewed over every word.

Processing Criticism

I handled that one much better than the first anonymous letter we received. The first one—another typed, unsigned letter—informed my husband that he prayed incorrectly and schooled him on the correct way. I read that one several times, studying the words carefully, ingesting them into my soul. The next time I went to church, I looked at every person and wondered if this one had written the note, if that one was the one who evaluated and judged everything my husband did. That letter, coming so early in our ministry, rattled me, causing me to shrink back a little in what God had called me to do.

In life, everyone has experienced silent offenses that threaten their joy and productivity, that breed cynicism and erect emotional walls. I daresay it happens ten times more in ministry. From where I stand as a pastor's wife, this is a make-it-or-break-it-all kind of issue; churches and ministry families rise and fall based on how the pastor and the pastor's wife handle the inevitable wounds that come along in ministry. Coupled with isolation or loneliness, ministry wives must often privately process criticism. Sometimes we even have to continue interacting (nicely) with people who have offended or hurt us or who continually complain about our husbands.

In church planting, our hurts are often compounded because the church plant is like our child—we fiercely protect it and deeply care about its success. Because of this deep attachment, we have a difficult time when friends leave the church, or sin and conflict affect the unity of the body. Being protective and sensitive regarding our husbands and the hard work they are doing, we are greatly offended when they are criticized or attacked.

And although we know hurts in ministry are inevitable, we are often surprised when they come. Our tendency is to believe that the church—certainly, our church—is immune to conflict or sin. But we shouldn't be surprised at all. Many of Paul's writings to the churches in the New Testament concern conflict, divisions, immorality, gossip, false teachings, mistrust of church leaders, disorder, and wolves among the sheep. Our modern-day churches experience the same, and as its leaders, there will be times that these same issues will affect our husbands and, in turn, affect us.

Opposition from Nonbelievers

In church planting, we will *definitely* experience opposition from unbelievers. As we shine light into dark places, the enemy will push back against our efforts.

We have been endlessly opposed by people in our neighborhood since the day we moved in. Neighbors complained when we canvassed the area, inviting them to join us for Bible study in our home. They complained when our Bible study/church outgrew our living room and we began meeting at the neighborhood community center on Sunday mornings. At homeowners meetings, we were publicly opposed and people called for our removal. Although we tried to be considerate, we received complaints about parking, noise, and that we were using the center for religious purposes. Finally, the detractors won out. On a Friday afternoon before our first major outreach event, we were told we could no longer meet in the community center, even for church the following Sunday. Being constantly opposed by people who were wary of our intentions was difficult, but we were unfazed because we trusted God to protect us and provide for us.

Jesus modeled what our response should be to persecution or opposition from unbelievers. He said:

We should expect opposition.
"I am sending you out like sheep among wolves. Therefore be as shrewd as snakes and as innocent as doves. Be on your guard against men; they will hand you over to the local councils and flog you in their synagogues." (Matthew 10:16 NIV)

We should not judge them
or expect from them what we expect from believers.
"Do not judge, or you too will be judged . . . Do not give dogs what is sacred; do not throw your pearls to pigs. If you do, they may trample them under their feet, and then turn and tear you to pieces." (Matthew 7:1, 6 NIV)

When a response is needed,
we should rely on the Spirit for what to say or do.
"On my account you will be brought before governors and kings as witnesses to them and to the Gentiles. But when they arrest you, do not worry about what to say or how to say it. At that time you will be given what to say, for it will not be you speaking, but the Spirit of your Father speaking through you." (Matthew 10:18–20 NIV)

Don't let opposition bother you.
Instead, count it a blessing when you are opposed.
"Blessed are you when people insult you, persecute you and falsely say all kinds of evil against you because of me. Rejoice and be glad, because great is your reward in heaven, for in the same way they persecuted the prophets who were before you." (Matthew 5:11–12 NIV)

Opposition from unbelievers is a form of spiritual warfare. The enemy often uses unbelievers as pawns to oppose the work of the Spirit. However, as we respond according to the Spirit's leadership, God can make good out of something that Satan intended for our harm.

> God used that opposition to move us where He wanted us.

God used the neighborhood opposition and our subsequent removal from the community center to do just that. The Sunday after we were asked to leave our meeting space, we had nowhere to gather other than under the tent we'd erected for our outreach event. Although it was raining, humid, and muddy underfoot, that day served to solidify our core group. The next week, after many months of waiting, we received word that our application to meet in a local school had been approved. Our forced move out of the community center and a sudden open door at the school came just before God blessed us with numerical growth, growth that wouldn't have been logistically possible in our first location. God used that opposition to move us where He wanted us.

Despite having moved the church to a location outside the neighborhood, we continue to receive opposition from within our neighborhood. Kyle and I seek to be loving, gentle, considerate, and accommodating, but also recognize that spiritual forces are at play. Jerry Rankin explains:

The reality is that we are in a battle . . . I often visit missionaries serving in places that are resistant to the gospel and see their discouragement. I ask, "What do you think God wants to do here?" They often reply, "I don't know. I would like to think He wants to bring these people to faith in Christ, but there is no evidence of that. We are just hoping for some response." Where did that attitude come from? . . . Who discourages us to believe contrary to what God has said, accepting obstacles to global evangelization, when that is clearly God's purpose? Who discourages us from a persistent witness because we are convinced it is futile and people will not respond? And even when we have success, it is often followed by dissension, disrupted by moral failure with our own minds constantly fighting defeatist attitudes. . . . However, we seldom think of this as spiritual warfare. It is so normal that we just brush off as human nature the lack of spiritual maturity, or weakness in our own faith and commitment. . . . We need to recognize the reality of spiritual warfare and that we have an enemy robbing us of a victorious life in order to deprive God of His glory in our lives.[17]

Opposition from Within

It's relatively easy to respond graciously when my husband faces opposition outside the church, but it is much more difficult when criticism comes from within. My initial response is typically anger or defensiveness, not graciousness.

As we all know, the church is not immune to the pain of conflict, sin, or broken relationships. As leaders, we are not immune to being misunderstood or criticized. Although our husbands more often bear the brunt of these things, as protective wives we tend to take the hurts to heart and let them affect us more than they ought. We may start keeping score, remembering wrongs and failing to forgive. We may allow little roots of bitterness to grow that, when harbored, develop into resentment and produce poisonous fruit. Full-blown bitterness causes us to retreat into ourselves, never again being fully vulnerable with others. If we don't weed out roots of bitterness, even when we've truly been wronged or treated unfairly, we become the sinner rather than just the sinned against. Its poison affects every area of our lives.

I speak from experience.

In my years of being a ministry wife, I have been hurt by the comments or actions of others. Generally, I can step back for a look at the big picture and see that the hurts were, in fact, unintentional or coming from an emotionally wounded person. There was a season, however, in which Kyle and I were hurt deeply from within our ministry. Over time, because of my hurt, I lost the ability to see the big picture or to trust God to bring truth to light. I never told anyone about what I was experiencing because I didn't want to multiply the problem, but anger planted seeds of bitterness in my heart, and I did not do anything to root it out. Instead, I let it fester. After all, I assured myself, I had done nothing wrong. It was my right to dwell on what had been done to us.

Seasoned church planting wives have learned how to appropriately deal with hurts in ministry

But that bitterness infected my heart, hanging like a cloud over my entire life, even the quiet moments I spent with the Lord and the intimate conversations I had with my husband. Before I knew it, I was no longer the sinned against but the sinner. Because I had let the bitterness grow unchecked, it was extremely difficult to remove. When I finally recognized what I had allowed and confessed my own sin, it still took *years* before the last roots were extracted. I resolved that never again would I allow bitterness to grow in my heart, no matter what I experience in ministry.

My prayer is for thick skin and a tender heart.

As I meet and observe seasoned church planting wives, I sense that those who are effective and joyful have one thing in common: they have learned how to appropriately deal with hurts in ministry. No matter what they have experienced, and no matter what it takes, they constantly rip out roots of bitterness and fight for joy. They've learned to forgive, because they know how disastrous unforgiveness is to the heart and how serious bitterness and anger are to God. He, after all, equates our anger toward others with murder: "You have heard that it was said to the people long ago, 'Do not murder, and anyone who murders will be subject to judgment.' But I tell you that anyone who is angry with his brother will be subject to judgment" (Matthew 5:21–22a NIV).

Anger and bitterness are serious to God because, left unchecked, they not only hold powerful control over the soul but also over the church when they abide in the hearts of leaders. Paul said it causes trouble, defiles the body, and keeps people from coming to salvation: "Make every effort to live in peace with all men and to be holy; without holiness no one will see the Lord. See to it that no one misses the grace of God and that no bitter root grows up to cause trouble and defile many" (Hebrews 12:14–15 NIV). Perhaps this is the enemy's greatest tactic with church planting wives and why we must not let bitter weeds grow in the tender soil of our hearts. Bitterness will certainly choke all the fruit-bearing plants in our homes and churches.

Sometimes rooting out bitterness and choosing to forgive slights takes a moment and other times it is a process of working through our hurts with God over time. Whatever it takes, we must root out bitterness in order to have joyful, healed hearts primed for ministry.

Why Forgive?

Our wounds sometimes seem too painful and our bitterness too great a hurdle. We don't want to see people who have hurt us week after week at church. We don't want to have to keep serving and putting ourselves out there, only to get hurt again. We don't want to be the "weird" church planters in our community, ostracized and opposed.

The only way we will be able to eradicate our hurts, fully forgive, and boldly press on is to know God's forgiveness for us and follow His example:

> Get rid of all bitterness, rage and anger, brawling and slander, along with every form of malice. Be kind and compassionate to one another, forgiving each other, **just as in Christ God forgave you.** (Ephesians 4:31–32 NIV)

God forgave us *all* trespasses. Who are we, who have been forgiven so much, to hold forgiveness from those who have offended us? Every time I am tempted to dwell on things that have offended me, including my most recent ministry hurts, the Spirit immediately reminds me of the parable of the unforgiving servant. The servant owed a large debt—

millions of dollars in today's currency—to his master, but the master, in his mercy, canceled the debt and let him go free. The servant then saw a man who owed him a small debt—about $20—and after demanding to be repaid immediately, threw the man in jail when he could not pay. "Then the master called the servant in. . . . 'I canceled all that debt of yours because you begged me to. Shouldn't you have had mercy on your fellow servant just as I had on you?'" (Matthew 18:21–35 NIV).

When we forgive, we release a debt that is rightfully owed to us. Forgiveness means we leave the baggage of hurt with Christ and walk away, knowing He will capably deal with the offender. Whether they ask for forgiveness or not, whether they acknowledge the hurt or not, whether they even know they hurt us or not, we leave it. We do it because we have been forgiven. We do it because if we hold on to it, then we become the offender in God's eyes.

> Jesus responded to offenders with sadness rather than anger.

Forgiveness is difficult because bitterness tells a conflicting but convincing story. Bitterness tells us that we must remember the offense because no one else will. It tells us that, by remembering, the offender is punished. It encourages us to cherish and recall every little hurt done toward us. But God says that when we forgive—when we leave it with Him—He deals with it perfectly, in the right way and in the right time. He doesn't need our help:

> Do not repay anyone evil for evil. Be careful to do what is right in the eyes of everybody. If it is possible, as far as it depends on you, live at peace with everyone. Do not take revenge, my friends, but leave room for God's wrath, for it is written: "It is mine to avenge; I will repay," says the Lord. On the contrary: "If your enemy is hungry, feed him; if he is thirsty, give him something to drink. In doing this, you will heap burning coals on his head." Do not be overcome by evil, but overcome evil with good. (Romans 12:17–21 NIV)

God forgave us through Christ, despite our offenses toward Him. Through Christ, He also modeled how to extend forgiveness to others.

Jesus endured a multitude of hurts. He was misunderstood, criticized, rejected, and killed. Untruths and misperceptions about His character and His mission went unchecked as the Pharisees slandered Him. His own friends didn't fully understand Him or what He was going to endure for them. They questioned Him and eventually deserted Him. Only Jesus saw the big picture because He looked through His Father's eyes.

Because He trusted His Father, He responded to offenders with sadness rather than anger. He saw the underlying pain and sin that caused people to hurt Him. He also saw the hardness of heart and selfish ambition that motivated the Pharisees and religious leaders. But He did not allow His circumstances to rule His emotions or distract Him from His singular purpose.

Jesus endured more unjust opposition than we ever will; therefore He knows how we feel when we are hurt. So we must "consider him who endured such opposition from sinful men, so that [we] will not grow weary and lose heart" (Hebrews 12:3 NIV). As we evaluate His response, we see a model for our own response to hurts. We are not perfect as Christ is, but God has given us the Spirit, a resource of supernatural wisdom and strength, to help us respond in the same manner that Jesus did.

The First Response

When I've been hurt, I immediately want to tell Kyle or privately stew about it for a while. I have discovered, however, that these responses only multiply my grievances and often lead to sin.

If my first response is to take my hurts to God, asking Him to search and test my heart, He gives me His perspective on the situation. He helps me see if I'm being too sensitive, if I'm forgetting that leaders are not immune to opposition or criticism, or if I'm trying to please people and my hurt is just my wounded pride. He also helps me consider if the criticism holds some truth, if there is a sin I need to confess, or if I have hurt the one who has hurt me.

Our initial fleshly response to criticism or conflict is often defensiveness, but we must take it to God. Is there truth in the criticism? Have we wronged our sister, intentionally or unintentionally? Have we sought to live at peace with everyone or have we shown conditional or selective love? Who is bringing the hurt: a trusted, loving friend out of genuine concern or a consistently critical person out of selfishness? Before we respond to the person who has hurt us or tell our husbands, we must first tune to God's assessment of our hearts and the situation at hand.

In one hurtful church planting situation, I knew that outwardly I had responded appropriately to the people who had offended us. But each time I prayed for the Lord's intervention on our behalf, He immediately stopped me, pointing to my prideful and unforgiving heart. Until I responded to God's prompting, until I forgave, God resisted my prayers. And, really, once I forgave, there wasn't much left to pray about. My focus in prayer returned to the ministry God had given me—not what He was or was not doing with those who hurt me.

Forgiveness is not usually instantaneous. Reminders of hurt often crop up, forcing us to choose whether we will release a debt all over again. Over time, as we root out bitterness and let the details of our hurts blur, our hearts will again grow soft toward ministry and the church, and even toward those who have hurt us.

The Prayerful Response

Sometimes, as we ask God to search our hearts, He requires an active response.

His ultimate goal in the midst of any hurt or difficulty is the sanctification of everyone involved. If we are mindful of this goal and let sanctification and grace inform our responses, we can trust the Spirit's leadership in working through our hurts.

If God reveals that we have wronged someone, even in the process of being wronged ourselves, we must confess our sin to God and to the person we have offended. A good confession will include three components: an "I was wrong when" statement, an acknowledgment of how the person may have felt about what you did ("It must have made you feel . . ."), and an opportunity to receive forgiveness ("Will you forgive me?").

God also often wants us to take on His perspective of the situation or of the person who has hurt us. As we pray, He shows us their underlying motivations for why they did what they did. He shows us if our wounds are "wounds of a friend," a trusted friend speaking from concern and love. Other times, He shows us that those who hurt others maliciously typically act out of their own deep hurts, giving us insight and compassion toward them rather than anger. He may show us their desperate desire for approval and how they have looked to us, the church planter's wife, for some value that we can't possibly give them. Whatever it is, as we choose God's perspective, the hurt loses some of its power and becomes less personal. Rather than getting angry, we feel sadness over the sin or the conflict, and we can show love to the person who has hurt us.

> Other ministry wives or friends outside the church can also provide perspective and encouragement.

Because we cannot always talk to others in the church about our hurts, our bitterness can be compounded. We easily feel caged within our hurts, isolated from the privilege of unhindered community that others enjoy. Our self-pity sometimes grants us permission to hold on to the bitterness, making it a secret, cherished "friend." However, we must not use our position as the church planter's wife as an excuse. The response God gives us will never be vindictive or slanderous toward others. At times, we will need to share our hurts with trusted women who can pray for us and give us wise counsel. Other ministry wives or friends outside the church can also provide perspective and encouragement. However, we must not use our hurts as an opportunity to slander, gossip, or gather others to our "side." According to Scripture, participating in these activities disqualifies us for future ministry as an elder's wife. In order to avoid multiplying hurts, sharing generalities about the situation with trusted advisors and asking for prayer may be best.

Finally, Jesus said that we should pray for those who have hurt us (Matthew 5:44). It is impossible to pray for someone while harboring unforgiveness toward them in our hearts. As you are faithful to pray for those who have hurt you, God will deal with any of your residual issues concerning the situation.

Cultivating Your Heart

Why should we expect opposition/criticism?

Have you been surprised by the source of any opposition/criticism you've encountered?

Why is it vital that we don't let bitterness choke us?

We can't always share our wounds, but God knows them intimately and heals them intimately. Ultimately, we can't protect ourselves from nicks, cuts, and wounds, but we can trust Him when they come. When we lay down any debts owed to us, in essence, we trust that God will deal rightly and justly with any offenses. We trust that His ways are right and perfect. We choose to care more about His will and His pleasure than what anyone does or does not say to us or about us.

God is the prodigal's Father, full of compassion, slow to anger, and quick in mercy. If we want to be like Him—not like the prodigal's brother standing at a distance, unable to forgive and harboring resentment—we must imitate His gracious response. As we continually root out weeds of bitterness and resentment under the Spirit's leadership, the Lord heals us and cultivates in us hearts of tenderness and compassion.

Consider the following verses as well as passages from the chapter.

Mark 4:16-17
Hebrews 12:14-15
Ephesians 6:18
Hebrews 12:1-3
Matthew 22:37-39

Interview with

Yvette
Mason

*Yvette is married to Eric, cofounder and lead pastor of Epiphany Fellowship
in Philadelphia, Pennsylvania. Epiphany started through home
Bible studies and then launched its first service in September 2006.
Yvette is a homeschooling mom to the couple's two energetic boys.*

What has been your greatest struggle(s) in church planting, and what have you learned through those struggles that might benefit another church planting wife?

Developing and maintaining authentic relationships. Once you become a pastor's wife, relationships change. You find it hard to determine whom you can trust, especially after people you choose to be vulnerable with have hurt you. A very wise and seasoned church planting pastor's wife told me that I should pray specifically that God would lead me to relationships, and He has. I have built relationships with our elders' wives, other women outside of Epiphany, and other church planting pastors' wives, in and out of our area.

Now does this mean that I won't be hurt? No, but as I have been in and out of situations of hurt in relationships with people I love, God has graced me to desire to be vulnerable again and know that "for those who love God ALL THINGS work together for good" (see Romans 8:28). He even uses the hurt of those relationships ending or failing to strengthen us and help us become conformed into His image. A verse I like to hold on to is 1 Peter 5:10: "And after you have suffered a little while, the God of all grace, who has called you to his eternal glory in Christ, will himself restore, confirm, strengthen, and establish you."

How do you respond when you or your husband is criticized or hurt?

Initially, we are shocked, disappointed, and weary. Then the Holy Spirit sobers us up and reminds us of the Word. These are some key passages we have meditated on:

1 Peter 4:12: "Beloved, do not be surprised at the fiery trial when it comes."

1 Peter 4:19: "Therefore let those who suffer according to God's will entrust their souls to a faithful Creator."

2 Corinthians 6:4: "As servants of God we commend ourselves in every way: by great endurance, in afflictions, hardships."

2 Chronicles 20:15: "The battle is not yours but God's."

Exodus 14:14: "The Lord will fight for you, and you have only to be silent."

Isn't that GREAT NEWS? So take the criticism in stride! He is working ALL THINGS out for His good! Hallelujah!

How do you support your husband when he is discouraged in his ministry?

When times of discouragement come, I pray more for him. I may ask him to share what's going on and I try to be a sounding board. I say try because I sometimes try to fix things, when all he may want is just a listening ear.

Also, I am trying to be a better servant, and I do so by asking him specifically what he needs. I don't try to figure it out on my own.

Sometimes he wants time with me alone. Sometimes he wants to be alone in the "man cave." Sometimes he wants to spend time with the boys and me together. But again, I try to ask him specifically, and if he is too weary to tell me (because there have been times where he was so weary, he couldn't even tell me what he needed), I pray and ask the Lord to show me.

What habits have you incorporated into your life that help you foster a love for God and for the ministry He's called you to?

I homeschool my boys, and have been in the process of developing worship time each day with them. We turn on one of our favorite worship songs, and blast it until the walls shake! We LOVE music and we love to worship, and God has led us to some great songs that have been vehicles to cause our hearts to turn toward things that concern His heart specifically. I have the tendency to be selfish. I know no one else struggles with this, right? So lately, I am sensing the Lord trying to steer my heart toward being more others-focused.

The ministry that the Lord has blessed us with serves a community where there is a large population of new Christians, college-aged, newly married, and those who are of a low-income status. Lately, I have been praying that God would give me compassion for the lost, just like Him.

It can be challenging to do this though, especially in an age where there is a lot of "entitlement" going on. The Lord is reminding me of where I was when I was their age in my faith and reminding me that during those times of "infant" faith, He graced me with people to walk with me as I matured. Trials, time, and maturity are all ways that the Lord uses to be conformed to His image, so I am just asking Him to give me the grace to apply a verse that is becoming my ongoing prayer: "And we urge you, brothers, admonish the idle, encourage the fainthearted, help the weak, be patient with them all" (1 Thessalonians 5:14).

My husband and I talk all the time about maintaining the "heart and eyes" of the church planter as we were at the beginning: missional, relational with outsiders, hospitable, outreach-minded. There is such a pull toward the comfortable, established-church mindset as we grow (read: inside-focused). How do you and your husband maintain the "heart and eyes" of the church planter as your church grows?

When Epiphany first started, my husband shared with me that at some point it was his desire for us to live in the neighborhood in which we would be serving. At first, I was skeptical. After all, we service an area that is known as "the bad lands." My husband was gracious enough to not immediately place his suburban-raised wife in this context, but he continued to pray that the Lord would change my heart. Over time, as I yielded to the will of the Father, my heart became softer toward the idea of living in our target area.

About two years ago, the Lord made that possible. We are now living about four blocks away from Epiphany's building. Since living here, the Lord has opened up many opportunities for us to build relationships with our neighbors and develop common ground for the gospel.

the Encouraged Heart

DEALING WITH DISCOURAGEMENT

Around the time our church plant turned two, I sat in church, completely discouraged and dejected. The enemy had gotten to me, turning my thoughts away from what God had done in our church and our community and toward what He had yet to do. However, my thoughts weren't a hopeful or prayerful anticipation of His future action. They were panic- and doubt-filled: *Where are You, God? What are You doing? Why have You not done things the way I want You to? Can I really trust You?* I ignored the evidence of His activity literally sitting all around me and saw only what appeared to be lacking.

I Was Discouraged When . . .

Discouragement has been the bane of my church planting existence. Before we planted, I considered that there would be difficult moments and setbacks, but I thought those times would be limited to the initial months or *maybe* the first year. The reality, however, is that I have been plagued by whole seasons of debilitating discouragement.

I was discouraged when, after one year of planting, the only other family with kids besides ours moved away.

I was discouraged when plans to move locations fell through.

I was discouraged when we couldn't find a worship leader.

I was discouraged when a good friend walked away from her husband and the Lord.

I was discouraged when our attempts at community outreach yielded few visible results.

I was discouraged when Kyle expressed his own discouragement.

I have been discouraged over how consistently hard the work is and how it will continue to be for the foreseeable future.

I don't need to go on because you know what I'm talking about. Being a church planting wife, you have your own discouragements. Because you know discouragement, you also know those moments of choice: belief and trust in God or giving in to despair.

As I sat in church that morning, I considered that choice. My discouragement stemmed from a lack of families in our church. We had an array of vibrant college students and young, married couples, but we were missing established families and wise elders who would add much-needed stability and maturity to our growing church. I longed for God's provision in this area, but He had not acted as I thought He should. Worse, I doubted that He cared enough about things to actually hear my plea and respond.

In that moment, as I considered what we were lacking, my lips could not move in worship. A wave of discouragement washed over me, causing my heart and my demeanor to drop. I knew I had a choice. I could continue thinking about what was lacking, which would create anxiety and doubt in my heart. Or, despite how I felt about the circumstances, I could take a moment to pray, ask God to provide what we were lacking, and leave my concerns with Him.

The enemy wants us to believe, however, that there is no choice, that discouragement is inevitable. In his attempts to hinder what the Spirit is doing in our church plants, if he can't get to our marriages, he uses discouragement more than anything else. He will use outside pressure—our circumstances—to draw us into discouragement. He will also use inside pressure—our flesh—to create doubt concerning God's character or provision for us.

Recently, I planned an early morning meeting with friends at our neighborhood clubhouse. I arrived first, turned the key to let myself in, and opened the door. Immediately, a sound pierced the air with a volume so loud that it surely woke the whole neighborhood. Stunned, I stared at the alarm, hoping it would magically turn off. But it didn't. Frantically and quite irrationally, I punched any number of combinations into the security keypad I could think of: my birthday, our wedding anniversary, as if the neighborhood association had only been thinking of me when they set the alarm code. Then I tried repeating numbers: 1111, 2222, 3333. The alarm seemed to grow louder and, with each blast, it accused me: Burglar! Intruder! Thief! I hadn't done anything wrong, but I felt as if I had. Gripped by panic and unsure of what to do, everything in me wanted to run away. In the end, let's just say that the alarm worked—*very* well—and that the policeman was nice.

> Once my attention was drawn onto frustrating circumstances, it was drawn away from truth, worship, and trust.

In that moment, although the alarm accused me, I was not an intruder nor did I need to act like one.

Satan uses similar tactics. He uses external and internal pressures as alarm bells that distract, cause panic, create irrational thoughts and feelings, and draw our attention away from truth, all in an attempt to discourage us. He makes things that are not true seem true and things that are true no longer seem true. Subtly, he throws us off course, hoping that we will become paralyzed by discouragement, or, even better, give up altogether.

For example, the Sunday I described above was a day that attendance was unusually low due to outside circumstances. I am generally not concerned with numbers, but I noticed it that day. This, combined with my own physical tiredness, set alarm bells off in my head. Once my attention was drawn onto frustrating circumstances, it was drawn away from truth, worship, and trust. I chose to listen to the alarm bell, which unleashed a torrent of doubt and fear in my heart.

But when I stopped to think about what I knew was true—God had called us to our city, He had built the church person by person, He had come through *many* times for us, and He was currently active among our people—I calmly turned off the alarm, refused to panic, released my burdens into God's hands, and returned to worship.

When I turned off the alarm in my heart, I did not *feel* encouraged. My circumstances did not instantly change. The setbacks and difficulties did not immediately disappear. But by remembering God's faithfulness, my heart settled and the panic subsided. I didn't know *how* God would work everything out, but I refused to get discouraged.

Waiting for It

There is an aspect of battling discouragement that involves waiting, whether it is waiting on God to act or waiting for our emotions to line up with truth.

Consider, for example, what Jesus' disciples experienced in the period between Christ's resurrection and the Holy Spirit's arrival. Before Jesus ascended to heaven, He assembled them together and commanded them not to depart from Jerusalem but to wait for the Holy Spirit. Surely their hands immediately shot up, eager with questions, but Jesus simply reiterated His promise and then left. And their waiting began. After what they had experienced throughout Jesus' life, death, resurrection, and ascension, I imagine that the longer they waited for this promised Helper, the more the alarm bells went off in their heads. Indeed, when the Holy Spirit rushed upon them, the size of the crowd had dwindled enough to fit into a small room.

Every time I read this passage, I wonder why the Holy Spirit didn't come immediately after Jesus' ascension. Why did He leave room for doubt and discouragement to creep in?

This seems to be God's typical mode of operation, when difficulty and waiting often precede His activity.

Hannah waited, wanted, and suffered before God gave her a child. After brokenness and barrenness, when the promised outcome seemed in jeopardy, she received God's gift.

Samuel anointed David as king long before David actually took the throne. Many of the Psalms describe his emotional anguish and his pleas for God to act on his behalf while being chased by a jealous Saul. Certainly he had reason to be discouraged, but he constantly turned off the alarm bells and fixed his eyes on God until God fulfilled His promise.

Consider also the overarching story of the Old Testament. All throughout, God weaves a story about a gift He plans to give His children—the Messiah. But for generations they waited, unsure of how the Gift would come and likely doubtful if God would actually give it at all.

Consider Lazarus. When Jesus learned of Lazarus's illness, He did not come immediately to heal him. Scripture says He did this out of love: "Now Jesus loved Martha and her sister and Lazarus. So, when He heard that he was sick, He stayed two more days in the place where He was" (John 11:5–6). He intentionally waited for Lazarus to die so God would get the glory of bringing him back to life.

God likes anticipation and it seems He has a purpose in making His children wait. Indeed, most if not all of His beloved servants—Abraham, Moses, Joseph, Esther, David, Paul, John—had to wait on God so long that they battled discouragement or doubt.

Why does God wait? Why does He allow opportunities for discouragement?

During those months of waiting, we second-guessed ourselves and worried that He would never give us clarity.

There is a mysterious value from heaven's point of view to being in the darkness of life and still choosing to believe in a God who seems to have forgotten us. Darkness is part of the school for the soul, to delve into what really matters. To put away all that is frivolous or vain and to sift through what really matters. When we are desperate, we are serious, focused on what life is all about, what He is all about.[18]

God designs waiting periods because He wants us to anticipate how and when He will fulfill His promises. After all, waiting with hope is the essence of faith, and we know that faith pleases God. However, we don't often see it that way. We don't like waiting, considering His not-yet answers to be a sign of our failures or weaknesses—or, worse, His failure or weakness.

In church planting, we have many seasons of waiting. As I look back, each of our church planting milestones were preceded by weeks or months of waiting for God's answer or action.

God called us to church planting before He told us where He wanted us to plant, so we spent many months waiting for Him to give us clarity and direction. During those months of waiting, we second-guessed ourselves and worried that He would never give us clarity.

Through supernatural circumstances, He told us, "Charlottesville!" and we waited for all the pieces to fall into place for us to sell our house, raise support, and move our family to a new place and new ministry. As we waited, I worried that we would not get to Charlottesville in time for our oldest to start school on the first day like everyone else. I wondered how we would be able to afford a house in a city with a high cost of living.

God came through on it all: the money was raised, the house sold, and our family moved into our new house a week before school started. Then we were eager to get started with our work in the city, but we had to wait on God to help us learn the culture, get to know people, and show us how to reach them.

We started a Bible study in our home, met people, and waited for God to grow our little group into a church. Despite our best efforts, we did not see fruit for a long time. I wondered if we had made a mistake or if we would actually successfully plant the church.

The Bible study on Sunday nights outgrew our home and our neighborhood community center, and we waited for God to open doors for a new location. He provided a perfect spot, not only as a Sunday meeting location but as a place where we could invest and serve.

For the first two years of planting, our worship team fluctuated wildly. We waited for God to provide our perfect worship leader. Some Sundays, I spent the entire worship time praying for God to bring that person to us. Seemingly out of nowhere, He sent a worship leader who is a perfect fit for us, our church, and our city.

We prayed for God to grow our church beyond one or two life stage groups, to bring us unbelievers, families, and potential elders. He has provided in each area.

Kyle and I prayerfully waited for the time when we could delegate ministries and responsibilities that we are not gifted for so we could operate more in our "sweet spots." That time has come.

We prayed that missions, church planting, outreach, and discipleship would become core values within our church. It has.

What have you and your husband had to wait for God to do or to answer? Most likely, those times of waiting have been difficult and discouraging, but have dramatically increased your trust in the Lord. That is His intention in the waiting period—that we would learn to trust Him. If we didn't have to wait, we might take credit for things that only God can do. Waiting, like the waiting Mary and Martha had to do when Lazarus died, brings glory to God because we know through our barrenness that we had nothing to do with the outcome.

Waiting Well

In church planting, there will be many, many opportunities for discouragement while we wait for the Lord to bring an increase or to change a person's heart or to draw someone to Himself. As Matthew Henry said, "Even the best saints are subject to faint when their troubles become grievous and tedious, their spirits are overwhelmed, and their flesh and heart fail. But then faith is a sovereign cordial; it keeps them from desponding under their burden and from despairing of relief, keeps them hoping, and praying, and waiting, and keeps up in them good thoughts of God."[19] How then do we wait well, feeding our faith rather than panicking with each alarm bell?

Psalm 27:13-14 (NIV) tells us how: "I am still confident of this: I will see the goodness of the Lord in the land of the living. Wait for the Lord; be strong and take heart and wait for the Lord."

We Must Be Strong

First, we are to be strong; some versions of Scripture say courageous. A soldier in heavy battle does not stand and let the battle come to him. He moves forward, fighting to the finish with a purpose in mind. His heart and his attention are not swayed by fear, but instead he is focused on completing his marching orders. Like a soldier advancing in battle, we must not dwell in our discouragement or let fear overwhelm us. We must take courage: do the next thing with the power He supplies, take a step forward in faith, keep our minds fixed on Him, and resolve to be unmoved by difficult circumstances or even our own emotions.

We Must Take Heart

Second, we must take heart. As we relate to the Lord, with our gaze fixed on Him, He strengthens and protects our hearts in our battle against discouragement. He aligns our emotions with truth. He reminds us that, although we cannot see His plan, He never stops working in us to will and act according to His good purpose. He also never stops working out everything for our good.

We Must Hope in the Lord

Finally, we are to hope in the Lord. Hope indicates confidence and assurance that He *will* act. With our hope in God, we can wait with eager anticipation to see how God will work in our lives and in our circumstances. When we have every reason to be discouraged, when uncertainty surrounds us, when we cannot guess the outcome, we can wait with joy, knowing that God is faithful. This is not reactive hope, this is proactive hope: we look for reasons to hope, we remind ourselves of God's faithfulness to us in the past, and we search Scripture for truth about God's trustworthiness. As we trust God, He fills us with courage.

Finding Encouragement

In 1 Samuel 30, David experienced a crisis. While he and his men fought the Philistines, another people group invaded their homes, burned their city, and carried away their wives and children. When David and his men returned home to find their homes charred and their families gone, they greatly grieved their losses. In their emotion, they turned on David, threatening to stone him. Having lost his own family and the respect of his men, David wept in distress. His next response, however, is what made him a great leader: "David strengthened himself in the Lord his God" (v. 6). I imagine David in an isolated place, on his knees, baring his pain to the Lord, and waiting expectantly for the Lord's strength to fill him, to show him how to respond.

As church planting wives, we have days when we can relate to

David, when it seems that our lives have been stripped of stability, comfort, or direction. We wonder how we got where we are or what God is doing. He seems far off and inactive. I have found that, in those waiting periods, He provides encouragement in often unexpected ways—if I have eyes to see it. Perhaps this is why we are to hope in the Lord—to anticipate His action so that we recognize His encouragement when it comes.

Where does His encouragement come from? How does the Lord typically encourage His children?

Encouraged through Scripture

His encouragement comes through Scripture. God not only pierces our hearts with His Word, but He also uses Scripture as a balm, comforting us, healing us, and urging us onward. You likely have favorites you return to; some of mine are at the end of the chapter.

We can be encouraged from Scripture that the work He sets us to is not in vain, and that He will not forget our faithfulness. During hard times, we can hold on to this truth and, following Abraham's example, not waver.

[He], contrary to hope, in hope believed, so that he became the father of many nations, according to what was spoken. . . . And not being weak in faith, he did not consider his own body, already dead, . . . and the deadness of Sarah's womb. He did not waver at the promise of God through unbelief, but was strengthened in faith, giving glory to God, and being fully convinced that what He had promised He was also able to perform. (Romans 4:18–21)

Encouraged through the Spirit

The Lord's encouragement also comes to us through the Spirit. Of course, the Spirit infuses our hearts with truth from Scripture, but He also uses circumstances or events as a means of pouring love into our hearts.

I live in a city of people who love expressing their passions through bumper stickers. There have been countless times that I have been driving, lost in anxious or despairing thoughts, and the Spirit has drawn my attention to a bumper sticker to speak truth to me. On an especially dark day, as I was losing a battle for truth regarding God's grace toward me, I pulled into a parking lot and noticed a bumper sticker on the car next to me: "Don't believe everything that you think." I have no idea why anyone would make a bumper sticker with that slogan or why anyone would choose it for their car, but the Holy Spirit used it that day to remind me that my emotions do not always speak truth to me. Because of that bumper sticker, the battle ended, and I praised God for His grace.

If we have eyes to see His activity, the Spirit consistently voices God's encouragement to us. Ask Him for encouragement and ask Him to help you recognize it when it comes. He will do it.

Encouraged through People

Finally, the Lord's encouragement comes through other people. I praise God for the body of Christ, for how quickly despair flees when other believers gather around. Just this week, after I expressed my discouragement to my good friend Melanie, she emailed me with what felt like providential words. She could have been writing to all church planting wives:

"Dear Christine, I am glad I know you. I am thankful for the people at our church. I am glad that you are willing to carry burdens with people and lift them up, even when it means you have to get messy in the process. I am sorry that it must be the case that the more the church grows, the more the burdens grow too, but there is so much positive growth, too.

"We talked about the Lykosh farm tonight and I thought there were some funny similarities for you two. They are growing food, and the closer they get to their goal, the more there is that can go wrong. Many more crops can fail, many more trees can succumb to disease or drought, many more chickens can overheat and die in the summer or get carelessly stepped on in the spring. In a weird way, every step they take toward their goal is a step toward failure, because they are that much more invested in the goal—more of their assets, their identity, their livelihood become entangled in their calling. So why do they keep investing more and more without proof that everything is going to work out? Apparently, it is primarily because they are faithful people doing the wild thing God has called them to do. So as they grow in that faithfulness to the calling, the things that can go wrong are so much greater, but how exciting to think about what it will be like when it all comes together!

> This is it! It's here! You're really doing it, and you have been prayed over; God has made the way for you!

"I think your awareness of the burdens and hurts in our community just reveals how closely you are tend-ing the harvest, and reveals your heart for your calling. I have to imagine that you and Kyle are somewhat underprepared. But this is it! It's here! You're really doing it, and you have been prayed over, God has made the way for you, and so now you work your fields until the work is done because what else could you possibly do after such a great investment? And I am sure that some years will yield little fruit and some years will be epic in their yield because that is just the way things seem to work in farming and ministry. But through it all, it is still your calling and still how God intends to bless you."

Melanie concluded her note with, "I can imagine that it would be difficult to see the big picture with church—what you are doing looks so impossibly big and crazy to me. Like when I look at people who can run 30 miles and I'm like, 'Were you made like that?!' But that is the funny thing—apparently you were made like 'that'—like how you are. And your ability to focus on the right things, simplify, pray with wisdom for people, protect and guide your family—that all seems so 'crazy' to me, just like picking up and moving across the country to start a farm is 'crazy' for someone else. And you really are going to rely on our community to fund your livelihood, and it really is going to work out. You really are going to grow into all the shepherding and discipling and hospitalitizing that God may have for you, and people really are going to grow closer to God and experience the joy of a life that finally feels worth living as a result.

"Just like tomato worms and end blossom rot are practically a result of growing tomatoes, tending people comes with a few signature pests, too. And you are going to become an expert worm squisher and slug getter and when people compliment you about how safe and beautiful your church congregation is, they'll have no idea what you have been doing to keep it that way."

Thankful We Said Yes

Standing among a throng of worshipers, I am overcome. *How did I get here? How did they get here? How did this happen?*

A moment ago, it seems, we lived a different life in a different place. Then God stirred up in us a crazy idea, almost too crazy to believe. Go, He said. In the spirit of Abraham and Sarah, pack it up, pack it in, and Go.

We had more questions than answers, but each step forward we took, attempting to discern and clarify what Go meant for us, He answered.

Us? Are You sure? Yes, start a church and ask others to go with you.

Where? Charlottesville, Virginia.

That's crazy. Are You sure? Yes, I'm sure.

Why? I have plans for you and your family there: to grow and change you, to use you to carry out a vision there, to bless you, to show you what faith is.

Are You absolutely sure? How? Child, walk by faith, not by sight and you will *really* see.

Among the throng, I am overcome with the clarity of God *with us.* Listening to the worshipers, my heart wells up in thanksgiving. The foreign has become familiar, the place has become a people, the land has become loved. I have tasted the fruit of faith and it is sweet. I have tasted God and, in this moment of clarity at what He has done, I am delighted in Him. He has shown me how to walk by faith and not by sight, how to *really* see.

Cultivating Your Heart

Read and meditate on these verses and the truths they convey. Add other favorites.

Our work in church planting is not in vain.

1 Corinthians 15:58: "Therefore, my beloved brethren, be steadfast, immovable, always abounding in the work of the Lord, knowing that your labor is not in vain in the Lord."

God sees and rewards our faithfulness.

Hebrews 6:10: "For God is not unjust to forget your work and labor of love which you have shown toward His name, in that you have ministered to the saints, and do minister."

In light of God's mercy, we should not give up.

Romans 12:1: "I beseech you therefore, brethren, by the mercies of God, that you present your bodies a living sacrifice, holy, acceptable to God, which is your reasonable service."

Hoping in God despite difficult circumstances is faith, which pleases Him.

Hebrews 11:6 NIV: "Without faith it is impossible to please God, because anyone who comes to him must believe that he exists and that he rewards those who earnestly seek him."

Know that you will see God's hand on your labor.

Psalm 27:13-14 NIV: "I am still confident of this: I will see the goodness of the Lord in the land of the living. Wait for the Lord; be strong and take heart and wait for the Lord."

Are You Willing?

Three years after the day I laid my head down on my pillow in our new home in a new state far from our families, wondering if something could be made out of nothing, God has done it. He has used His people, so broken and weak, to bring life to a spiritually dark place.

Every so often, I stand in front of my wedding vows, hanging framed on the wall. Just as when I wrote the words, my heart stops on one line.

I vow to support the ministry that God gives you.

Clearly, my support and affirmation of my husband's ministry has been vital. And clearly, God has moved powerfully around and among us.

But the work is far from complete. The Lord is still calling on me to move forward in faith—loving, serving, discipling, and leading. Daily He asks for my heart, that He might cultivate it so as to produce fruit.

Am I willing?

Are *you* willing?

Sisters, God is for you, and my prayers are with you as you fulfill the calling He has placed on your life. Let us continue to labor together for the gospel alongside our husbands with great faith, joyful sacrifice, and service. "For this reason I bow my knees to the Father of our Lord Jesus Christ . . . that He would grant you, according to the riches of His glory, to be strengthened with might through His Spirit in the inner man" (Ephesians 3:14–16).

a Word *to* Those Preparing *to* Church Plant

On my blog, I often get questions from women whose husbands are considering church planting or are in the final preparation stages before planting. If you are one of those women, I hope this book gives you an accurate picture of the joys and difficulties of church planting, but I also know that you have questions, challenges, and fears unique to this time of prayer and preparation. This section is for you. I also invite you to visit my blog (www.gracecoversme.com) for additional and ongoing help and encouragement as you plunge in.

My husband and I are considering church planting.
How do I know for sure if this is what God is calling us to do?

You and your husband are the only ones who can answer this question fully. In general, God speaks through circumstances, people, His Word, and by His Spirit. Regarding your call to church planting, He will use those same avenues.

For us, He used all of these avenues.

Two years prior to church planting, we began noticing our hearts changing. We were working with college students, but we both recognized that God was growing in us a heart and passion for the larger church. It felt like Kyle was growing out of his leadership "box" and that God was preparing him for a greater challenge. At the same time, our hearts were growing for reaching people with the gospel and wanting to influence others to do the same.

God used people as well. Other church planters began encouraging Kyle to consider this type of work. The church we were serving in became more interested in church planting, and the pastor encouraged Kyle's interest. When we began considering church planting, we asked for prayer from trusted friends and family, and they affirmed this calling in us.

In chapter 6 of this book, I share the "snapshots" of how God spoke to me by His Spirit and through His Word. After about nine months of prayer, discussion, assessment, and counsel, I knew without a doubt that we were supposed to church plant. That did not mean that I didn't have questions, fears, or struggles. But I knew that we would be disobedient if we stayed where we were.

One of the most helpful things we did as we were discerning the call was attend a church planting conference. These conferences give you a realistic picture of what the work is and how it is done. I'd like to share with you how God used the conference in my life specifically, especially if you're thinking:

My husband wants to church plant, but I'm not so sure.

As I mentioned in chapter 3, during the church planting boot camp we attended in 2007, Kyle and I knew God was speaking to us, but we were full of questions. Kyle questioned whether or not he was a church planter. I saw it instantly. I questioned whether or not I could be a church planting wife. He saw things in me that I couldn't see.

Full of trepidation and uncertainty, we *both* affirmed to each other that we were available to God if this is what He wanted for us.

Without a doubt, both a husband and a wife must be on board. The church planting wife is as vital to the health of the plant as the church planter. Because of this, there must be honest conversation between the two of you before you jump in.

If your husband wants to church plant, you can ask certain things. Has he sought counsel from experienced church planters and/or mentors? Does he meet the qualifications of an elder? Can he embrace and execute the requirements of a church planting elder? Does he see difficult things through? Is he faithful in leading your marriage and your family? You know the answers better than anyone else, and you have a responsibility to speak into his life if you have hesitations. You also have a responsibility as his God-given wife to affirm his calling and help him fulfill it, even if it's something that scares you.

If he is the man for the job and God is leading both of you down this road, then there are questions you must ask yourself. If you have hesitations, why? Are you informed about what church planting entails? Are you willing to sacrifice and serve in order to help your husband? Are your fears valid? Generally, wives are fearful of the instability, insecurity, and demands of church planting. I had fears and doubts, too; otherwise it wouldn't have been an act of faith. Fear is not a reason to hinder your husband from fulfilling his call. If God calls you to something, He *will* provide what you need. If God is calling you and your husband to church, you *must* get on board, not because you are submitting to your husband but because you are submitting to the Lord.

That is how you know: you ask Him with a heart to obey.

We feel certain that God is calling us to church plant.
How do we discern where?

When I speak of our church or our ministry, I find myself using plural pronouns. We moved to Charlottesville. We planted a church. Am I a church planter? In the sense of carrying the load and leading the church, I am not. But in the sense of most everything else—time, effort, concern, and goals—I am. I am not just a church planter's wife; I am a church *planting* wife.

I say all this simply to reiterate what I said to the previous question: this is a together calling. This is my husband's job and calling, but it's my calling too, because he could not fulfill his calling without my full support, without my being behind him and beside him.

You certainly must be asking, "How is this answering the question?" Because it is vital that we know God's call to church plant both for our husbands and for ourselves. I simply cannot say it enough. The *where* is nowhere close to as important as the *certainty of the calling to go.*

We knew we were supposed to plant a church before we knew where. We felt certain about this calling because over a period of time my husband and I both felt an atypical unrest about where we were in life. Everywhere we turned, we heard sermons or talks about the church; God seemed to urge us to expand our horizons regarding the local and global church. At the same time, different and unconnected individuals with experience in church planting encouraged Kyle to consider church planting. We attended the boot camp I mentioned previously, and when I heard Mark Driscoll describe my husband, I felt a little fear rise up in me. Perhaps God was really up to something. Surely He was going to use my husband, but I doubted whether He could use me.

That weekend, Kyle and I talked for hours, sensing God's hand directing our steps. A few weeks later, we took a personal retreat. We spent that time talking together and asking God for confirmation that He was indeed calling us to plant a church. And when He did, we talked about tentative places where He might be calling us. We had no idea and no leading, but we left the weekend assured of our general calling.

Over the few months we prayed. A lot. Over and over, we questioned how we were supposed to know where God was calling us to plant a church. Over and over, we prayed. And waited. And worried. And prayed some more.

Wise counselors suggested that we consider where we would enjoy raising our family, where needs exist, and where the needs of the city match our passions and gifts. Using those suggestions, we easily narrowed down our criteria. We wanted to plant a church outside of the Bible Belt, in a college town with an influential university, in a midsize city close to metropolitan areas, and in an area where we could reach college students, young people, and growing families. With that in mind, we pinpointed college towns on a map of the United States, which we hung on our bathroom mirror and prayed over daily.

Just after Christmas in 2007, as we drove home from visiting family, our conversation again turned to the "wheres" and "hows" of this crazy church planting idea stuck in our heads. As we listed universities and college towns, we mulled over each one, hoping for some flash of inspiration or intrigue. Virginia Tech popped to mind and then a question: "Where is the University of Virginia?"

When we got home, I Googled it, found the answer, and then went straight to Wikipedia to research this Charlottesville place I knew nothing about. We looked at the pictures, read about the University of Virginia, and went to bed.

The next day, Kyle came home from work and, as we sat down for dinner, said, "I can't stop thinking about Charlottesville." All day, I had been thinking about the pictures I'd seen and the words I had read about the city, but I had also thought about how crazy it was to think God would call us to a city through Wikipedia. "Funny," I said, "I can't stop thinking about it either."

We decided that Kyle would call our denomination in Virginia just so we could get the crazy idea out of our heads and move on. But when he did, the church planting strategist said, "We've been praying for two years that a young couple would move here to plant a church reaching UVA students and young people." Well, as you can imagine, that stopped us in our tracks. They invited us to visit Charlottesville, which we did, and immediately fell in love with the place.

As our plane lifted off to take us out of Virginia a few days later, I vividly remember thinking that we were leaving our home.

When we got home, however, we began to count the cost. Were we absolutely *sure*? I had just given birth to our third child. We needed to be *sure* before we left a stable income and moved our children across the country, far away from extended family. Of course, the element of faith in church planting takes away the "for sures," but God graciously gave us several confirmations that couldn't be ignored.

When we started recruiting people to go with us as a core team, one of our college students told us that two students who had been leaders in our ministry before graduating, marrying, and moving away were moving to Charlottesville for a job. What?! I couldn't believe my ears.

Second, Kyle and his best friend Bill, a youth minister in Ft. Worth, had always talked about doing ministry together. Before we knew the location, Kyle told Bill about our plans and asked him to consider doing it with us. Bill was hesitant, but continued praying about it. When we settled on Charlottesville, Kyle called Bill and told him where we were going, pressing him to join us. Bill grew silent. Then: "Charlottesville, Virginia? You've got to be kidding me." He went on to tell Kyle that he had toured tons of colleges with his parents during high school. One of the schools was UVA and he had loved Charlottesville so much that he had jokingly talked with his buddies during college about starting a church in the city someday. Somehow Kyle had never been in on those conversations. Bill couldn't shake the coincidence, prayed about it, and soon signed on to go.

The point of my telling this story is not to say that God will lead you in a similar way. The point is that God will lead you as you wait on Him. My advice is to wait on Him expectantly through prayer, reading Scripture, and seeking wise counsel. As George Muller learned,

> Continued uncertainty as to one's course is a reason for continued waiting. . . . The flesh is impatient of all delay, both in decision and action; hence all carnal choices are immature and premature, and all carnal courses are mistaken and unspiritual. God is often moved to delay that we may be led to pray, and even the answers to prayer are deferred that the natural and carnal spirit may be kept in check and self-will may bow before the will of God . . . he who would work with God must first wait on Him and wait for Him.[20]

If you cultivate a tender heart toward God and are *willing to go*, you can't miss His leading.

As the wife of the church planter, what will my role in the church look like?

First and foremost, you are a disciple of Christ, a wife, and, if you have children, a mother. As challenging as it may be, these roles must remain priorities throughout the church planting process.

But even with these as your priorities, you will be called on to help your husband in countless ways.

In the beginning stages of the church plant, you will be a generalist. You may be asked to do any and all of the following: starting and coordinating ministries such as children's or hospitality, graphic and website design, worship, making and printing bulletins, leading a small group, starting a women's ministry, counseling, calling visitors, hosting visitors, meetings, small group, fellowships, and, if you're like me, holding church in your home.

By year three or four, you may be able to become more of a specialist. You will be able to delegate ministries that do not fit within your giftedness and to focus on those that you truly enjoy.

I have found that in every stage of the church, aside from being a disciple, wife, and mother, my primary role has been hospitality: building relationships, meeting with people, welcoming visitors at church on Sundays, having people over, hosting showers, leading small groups, and hosting informal church gatherings in our home. I think you can expect your role to be much the same, especially if your church does not own or lease a building.

What should I expect in the first year or two of church planting?

At the time God called us to church plant, Kyle was a college and missions pastor at a large established church in Texas. We didn't have any church planting experience, so we had no idea what we were getting into. But we were gung ho, filled with faith, and excited about our church planting adventure.

It took about a day to realize that it was going to be harder than I had expected. I didn't expect my gung ho faith to give way so quickly to fear, discouragement, and doubt. I also didn't anticipate that, after three years, I would be such a radically changed person.

Here are some things you can expect as you plant:

It's a marathon, not a sprint. Each year of church planting is like running a marathon—it's long, exhausting, and pushing your limits. Church planting will require your complete dependence on God for the sustenance you need to cross the finish line each year and then pick right back up and run for another year. Knowing this going in, you must pace yourself.

You will grow the hard way. You can expect to grow in ways that only come through difficulty, stepping outside your comfort zone, and the testing of your faith. I have gone from relating to God in a good-girl, checklist kind of way to knowing my utter need for Him. I now completely understand John 15, that I cannot do anything apart from Him. No amount of work, charisma, or planning can make a seed sprout. He alone causes growth—in me and in the church.

Your marriage will be challenged. Before we planted, I read that even strong marriages are tested through church planting. Small divisions or strife becomes great chasms because of the stress church planting places on a marriage. My husband and I had a strong marriage before church planting, so I assumed that we wouldn't be affected by it. I was wrong. Church planting brought problems to the surface that had not been problems before, things like communication and conflict resolution. Thankfully, we have faced those things head-on and I would say that, having gone through the fire of church planting, we have a stronger and more intimate marriage than ever before. It's important to have a plan in place for you and your husband to communicate, plan, schedule, rest, and spend time together as a couple and a family.

Your husband will need you and your full support. Kyle is not the type to get stressed or worried. He is pretty laid-back and if I do say so myself, a great leader. He entered church planting with experience and a personality and giftedness well suited for this work. I didn't expect to see him get discouraged or fearful, but there have been many times when my job has been to earnestly encourage him, pray for him, and support him in his ministry. This is tough work and sometimes it will be hard for you to watch what it takes out of your husband.

You will experience opposition. Some people just won't understand what you're doing or will think you're weird. Some who will tell you about all the church plants they've seen fail in your city. But you can also expect spiritual opposition. I knew *about* spiritual warfare before church planting, but I have never *experienced* it like this before. I highly recommend reading about and studying spiritual warfare before you church plant.

It will be great for your kids. I love how church planting has affected our kids (when we began, they were five, two, and six months). They are known and loved by people in the church, especially those who were in the core group. They have been involved in outreach to our community. Most importantly, we get to talk to them about what we're doing and why, which sparks lots of great conversation about faith.

Relationships will be the key. I cannot emphasize enough that relationships and hospitality will be key to your church plant's success. Our growth has happened one relationship at a time, and sometimes it's taken years of building relationships with people before they ever set foot in our church. Expect to open your home countless times as a tool for ministry.

It is worth it. There will be times you'll think, *What have I gotten myself into?* Church planting is hard work, the hardest ministry work I've ever been a part of. But it's so worth it! I could fill up pages and pages of my journal (and I have!) with the things I've seen God do. Most people don't get such a front-row seat to the action, but you and I do, and that's something to be thankful for.

How can I best prepare for what lies ahead?

In some ways, preparing to church plant is like getting engaged: you're moving toward the big day, you really have no idea what to expect other than what people have told you from their own experience, and you're in the midst of a lot of planning, preparation, excitement, and uncertainty.

You know how people tend to put more effort into planning the wedding than preparing for the actual marriage? Don't make that same mistake when it comes to church planting. It's easy to focus entirely on getting the house sold, raising financial support, creating a prospectus, and making logistical plans for our children without ever considering what will sustain our souls, faith, marriages, families, and fledgling churches a month or year or four years down the road.

Looking back on the six months prior to our plant, the following are the things I did that prepared me or, more accurately, the following are the things I *wished* I had done that might have eased my transition from established church to church plant:

Develop a consistent time in the Word and prayer. I cannot emphasize this enough. There will be times in church planting when you are desperate for encouragement, the voice of God, the movement of God, help, energy, or a renewed faith. You won't be able to rely on your husband for those things because he will be just as desperate as you. You may not yet have a church body to turn to because, hey, that's what you're trying to build. Your family and friends may be physically and experientially miles away. The help and sustenance you crave can only and will only be found in God. The Word is your lifeline to Him. Teach yourself to crave the Word, drench yourself in it, and learn to depend on God for everything that you need. (Start reading daily in Acts because you will soon feel like you're living a chapter out of that book.)

Feed your faith. As you prepare to plant, you will have innumerable opportunities to doubt, fear, worry, resist God, and even back out altogether. The answer? Faith. Exercise it by battling the doubts and fears that rage inside of you. Dig into the Word for truth about God's character that gives you a solid foundation to stand on. At every turn, choose to believe God and to trust that He will fulfill what He's called you to do. "Trust in the Lord, and do good; Dwell in the land, and feed on His faithfulness" (Psalm 37:3).

Read helpful resources. Fill your mind with the Word but also with good resources that challenge and inspire your faith. For me, this means reading good biographies of men and women who proclaimed Christ, such as *The Hiding Place* (Corrie ten Boom); *Faithful Women and Their Extraordinary God* (Noel Piper); *Peace Child* (Don Richardson); *Bonhoeffer: Pastor, Martyr, Prophet, Spy* (Eric Metaxas); *And The Word Came with Power* (Joanne Shetler); *A Chance to Die* (Elisabeth Elliot); and *Living Sacrifice* (Helen Roseveare). In preparation, also read church planting books right alongside your husband so you know what to expect and what this requires for him. My husband recommends *Planting Missional Churches* (Ed Stetzer); *Church Planter* (Darrin Patrick); *Confessions of a Reformission Rev* and *Radical Reformission* (Mark Driscoll); and *Launch: Starting a New Church from Scratch* (Nelson Searcy and Kerrick Thomas).

Clarify and confirm your calling. During your time of preparation, truly nail down your calling. When everyone stops cheering and patting you on the back as they send you off to church plant, your clear calling from God will sustain you. Also, check your motives for church planting before they are tested by trials, hard work, and setbacks. Make sure you're doing it because God is calling you, not because you're frustrated in your current situation. Church planting is not the answer to your hurts or your frustrations; in fact, it will only exacerbate unresolved issues in your heart.

Journal. As God clarifies and confirms your calling, write everything down. Record how God answers prayer, how He confirms your calling, what verses He is using to speak to your fears and concerns, and any and all victories you experience.

Gather people. Ask people for prayer support and tell them honestly what you need prayer for. If possible, gather people to go with you. Finally, if possible, connect with other wise church planting wives who have gone before you so that you can ask questions and share your concerns. Leading and Loving It, an online ministry for ministry wives, provides just such an opportunity.

Practice what you're about to do. Church planting is all about people, people, people. If you're not all about people, people, people, you need to start being all about people, people, people. Talk to people, ask good questions of people, steer conversations in a spiritual direction, socialize with nonbelievers, get to know your neighbors, practice hospitality, or join a community organization. In other words, get outside the walls of the church. You will not have those walls in a few short months.

Learn about key church planting concepts. The sower and grower principles found in 1 Corinthians 3:5–8 detail that God is responsible for church growth, while we are responsible for planting and watering seeds. John 15 says that we can't do anything unless we abide in the Vine. Ephesians 6 speaks about intense spiritual warfare. Learn these, memorize them, and put them into practice because they affect how you plant and how you respond to the difficulties of church planting.

Finally, dream. You are about to get to build a church from the ground up. You and your husband will implant your DNA into this church and shape this church more than anyone else. That's a great responsibility, but it's also an incredible opportunity to impact a specific people and a specific community with the gospel.

Dream big!

For more, including good resources for church planting,
please visit my blog: www.gracecoversme.com.

Notes

1. Matthew Henry, "Proverbs 4," *Complete Commentary on the Bible*, biblestudytools.com.

2. Oswald Chambers, *My Utmost for His Highest*, classic ed. (Uhrichsville, OH: Barbour), October 3.

3. Frank E. Gaebelein, ed., *The Expositor's Bible Commentary: John and Acts* (Volume 9) (Grand Rapids: Zondervan, 1981), 151.

4. Oswald Chambers, February 9.

5. Douglas Wilson, *Reforming Marriage* (Moscow, ID.: Canon Press, 1995), 16.

6. Shari Thomas, "A Study of PCA Church Planter Spouse Stress and Satisfaction Levels," *Mission North America: Presbyterian Church in America*.

7. Deitrich Bonhoeffer, *Life Together* (New York City: Harper & Row Publishers, Inc., 1954), 20.

8. Oswald Chambers, February 5.

9. Nancy Leigh DeMoss, *Brokenness: The Heart God Revives* (Chicago: Moody, 2008), 60.

10. Dr. Helen Roseveare, *Living Sacrifice: Willing to Be Whittled as an Arrow* (Great Britain: Christian Focus Publications), 31–32.

11. Elisabeth Elliot, *A Chance to Die: The Life and Legacy of Amy Carmichael* (Grand Rapids: Revell, 2005), 183.

12. Thomas White, "Courage in the Face of Fear," *Southwestern News* (summer 2010):13.

13. Shari Thomas, "A Study of PCA Church Planter Spouse Stress and Satisfaction Levels."

14. Ibid.

15. Paul Miller, *The Praying Life* (Colorado Springs: NavPress, 2009), 23.

16. A. W. Tozer, *The Pursuit of God* (Camp Hill, PA: Christian Publications, Inc., 1993), 75–76.

17. Jerry Rankin, *Spiritual Warfare: The Battle for God's Glory* (Nashville: Broadman & Holman), 13–14.

18. Sally Clarkson, "Walking through Soul-Darkness," *ITakeJoy.com*. 05/04/2011. www. itakejoy.com/walking-through-soul-darkness/.

19. Matthew Henry, "Commentary on Psalm 27," blueletterbible.org.

20. Arthur Pierson, *George Muller of Bristol and His Witness to a Prayer-Hearing God* (London: Baker and Taylor Co., 1899), 25–26.

Acknowledgments

If I have anything worthwhile to offer in this book, it's because of Jesus and because He has taught me about Himself, about myself, and about true ministry through our church planting adventures. He has used church planting more than anything else to refine me, and I am forever grateful.

There is no one who has championed me more in life and in writing than my husband. Kyle, you are a man among men, a gifted leader, and an excellent husband and father. Thank you for sacrificing for me so that I could pursue my passions and believing in me when I wanted to give up. Oh, and thank you for making me a church planting wife!

I have loved what church planting has meant for my boys: a church that knows and loves them, countless opportunities to serve people, and a "together" adventure. Will, Reese, and Luke, you are treasures to me. I'm thankful that you celebrate me just as much as I get to celebrate you. It is my constant prayer that you will know the joy of following Jesus.

Sometimes I look around at church on Sunday mornings and wonder how we got to be so blessed. Thank you, Charlottesville Community Church, for loving our family, loving our city, and letting me write freely about ministry on my blog without it being awkward for either of us.

Our families have always been supportive of us, even when we moved across the country from them to plant a church. Thank you Mom, Dad, Sarah, and Travis, as well as my family-in-love: Paula, Ray, Chris, and Jenifer.

My girlfriends have encouraged me in life, ministry, and writing at some of my lowest times, asked good questions (my love language!), and spurred my faith. Jo, Emily, and Jenny, God has especially used you. Marylyn, thank you isn't enough for the sister you've been to me throughout this church planting and writing journey. Friend, I'm grateful for your editing expertise, your vulnerability, your timely words, and for encouraging me to keep writing.

Grace Covers Me readers: without you, this would never have happened. Thank you.

Thank you also to the church planting wives who shared their wisdom with me: Lauren Chandler, Jenn Carter, Lora Batterson, Shauna Pilgreen, Yvette Mason, Brandi Wilson, Ginger Vassar, Jen Hatmaker, Lori McDonald, Jenn Atwell, and Amanda Jones.

I am grateful that this book is now in the hands of women who have long needed resources, encouragement, and an affirmation of their unique and vital calling. Les Stobbe, my formidable literary agent, thank you for first seeing the value of this resource, and Barnabas Piper, thank you for advocating for it at Moody.

The team at Moody has been a delight to work with. Barnabas Piper, Duane Sherman, Johanna Hensler, Pam Pugh, and Brittany Biggs: Thank you for your efforts on my behalf and on behalf of church planting wives everywhere.